PIANO LESSONS: IN 1 DAY

4 Manuscripts in 1 Book, Including: How to Play Piano, Music Theory, How to Read Music and How to Play Chords

Preston Hoffman

More by Preston Hoffman

Discover all books from the Music Best Seller Series by Preston Hoffman at:

bit.ly/preston-hoffman

Book 1: *Music Theory*

Book 2: *How to Read Music*

Book 3: *How to Play Guitar*

Book 4: *How to Play Ukulele*

Book 5: *How to Play Piano*

Book 6: *How to Play Chords*

Book 7: *How to Play Scales*

Themed book bundles available at discounted prices:

bit.ly/preston-hoffman

Table of Contents

HOW TO PLAY PIANO: IN 1 DAY 5

MUSIC THEORY: FOR BEGINNERS 70

HOW TO READ MUSIC: IN 1 DAY 156

HOW TO PLAY CHORDS: IN 1 DAY 216

HOW TO PLAY
PIANO
IN 1 DAY
The Only 7 Exercises You Need to
Learn Piano Theory, Piano Technique
and Piano Sheet Music Today
PRESTON HOFFMAN

BOOK 1

HOW TO PLAY PIANO: IN 1 DAY

The Only 7 Exercises You Need to Learn Piano Theory, Piano Technique and Piano Sheet Music Today

Preston Hoffman

Table of Contents

Introduction.. 8

Chapter One: The Keyboard and Keys 10

Chapter Two: The Pedals.. 16

Chapter Three: Reading Sheet Music 20

Chapter Four: Practising Scales 33

Chapter Five: Adding in Chords 39

Chapter Six: Sharps and Flats 49

Chapter Seven: It's All About the Timing................................ 53

Final Words.. 68

Introduction

Have you always wanted to learn to play the piano? Have you been hesitant about doing so because of the thought of having to spend endless hours practicing? Maybe you took some lessons but gave up because it was too hard.

What if there was a much easier way? What if I were to tell you that you could learn all the basics in seven simple lessons and that you could learn to play a proper tune in less than a day?

Does that sound a little too good to be true? Here are a couple more facts for you – playing the piano is not that complicated. It's just that the way that we are traditionally taught to play is a lot more complicated than it needs to be. Normally, you have to start by learning one note at a time, and have to learn all the theory before you get to actually start practicing what you have learned.

There is a lot of work to do before you even get close to seeing real results and that can be very disheartening.

What we do in this book is to break it down for you into simple but essential steps. You will learn the basics of music theory quickly and easily and will be able to play your first tune within hours. This will give you the motivation to carry on and keep practicing.

Will this book turn you into a maestro? No, but then it is not designed to do that. It will, however, get you started and teach you the foundations that you can build on.

You'll get to show your friends and family just how smart you are by being able to play your favorite songs – and save yourself a bundle in sheet music too.

If you are looking for an excellent introduction to playing the piano, this is the book for you. If you decide to carry on learning from there, this gives you a solid base to do that as well.

Chapter One: The Keyboard and Keys

In this chapter, you will learn about all the keys on the keyboard. This is the first step in our seven-point plan to teach you how to play the piano.

Your piano keyboard will look like this:

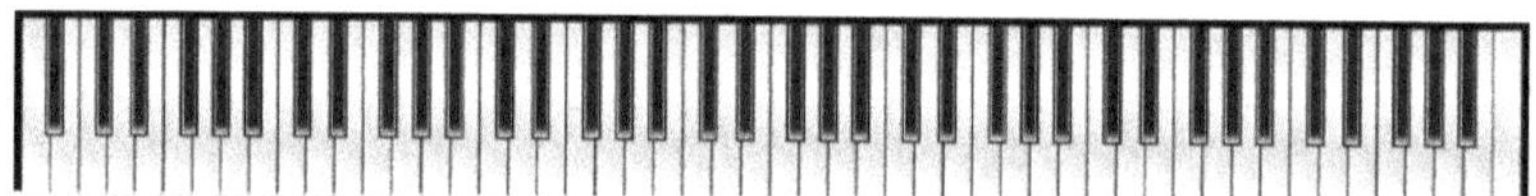

Looking down at the keyboard for the first time can be a bit intimidating. The keyboard is made up of a set of 52 white long keys, and a set of 36 shorter, more raised black keys. You should have 88 keys in total. (Some older pianos have smaller keyboards.)

Have a look at the diagram below – it is a smaller section of the keyboard, and contains all the basic information that you need to know. Once you get to know this information, you can basically apply it to the rest of the keyboard.

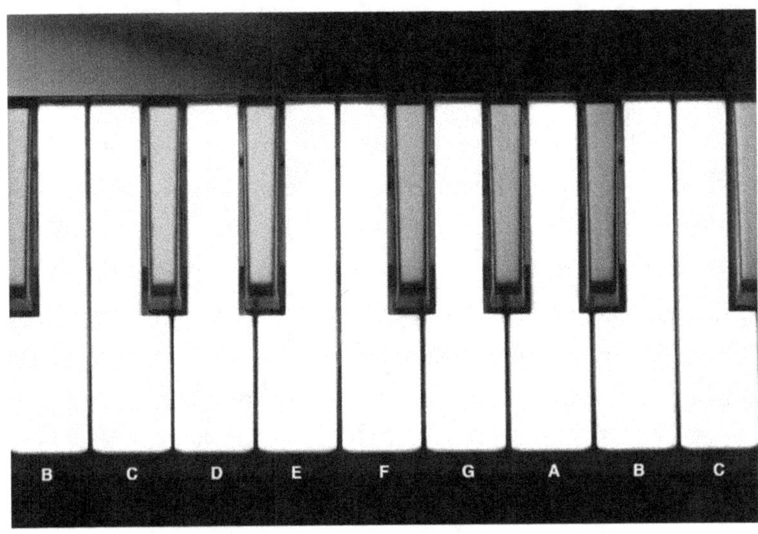

The White Keys

The white keys, as shown above, each play a particular note in music. These are named for the first seven letters of the alphabet – A through to G. There are a lot more keys than there are notes, so the letters are repeated over and over again. So, starting at the very left edge of the keyboard, you start with the letter A. The repetition makes it a lot easier – there are the same seven notes over and over again.

The next key represents the "B" chord, and so on, until you get to the key after the "G" chord. Then the keys start at "A" again. Each set represents one octave.

So, do you have to sit down and count each key from the start to determine which letter it represents? Fortunately, there is an easier way, and that is part of the reason that we have the black keys.

The black keys are divided into groupings of twos (twins) – marked in green on the diagram above or threes (triplets) – marked in red on the diagram above. The "C" note is always to the left of a set of twins. The "F" note is always to the left of a set of the triplets. To remember this more easily, you can think of the "C" as having two points to it and the "F" as having three points to it. From there, it is easy enough to fill in the remaining letters.

Whereabouts the keys are positioned on the board indicates how high or low the note is. The lowest notes are on the left, and you move up the scales as you move over to the right.

Quick Exercise: Play each key now and see how different they all sound. Find each of the "C" keys on the keyboard. Follow with all of the "D" keys and so on. Then play the following notes on any set of the keys:

B, D, B, E, D, B.

Do you recognize the tune at all? Does it remind you of when you were a kid? It should – it's the start of "It's Raining, It's Pouring." Well done, you have just played a tune without a single music sheet in sight. Didn't I tell you that this was going to be easy?

Play it again in a different octave so that you can hear how it sounds higher or lower. Repeat on all the different octaves to note the differences in sound.

The Black Keys

The black keys are different musical notes to the white keys. Play them, and you will notice a distinct difference. The names of these keys are also the same letters of the alphabet and take on the names of the white keys nearest them. The distinction is that keys to the left of the white key are known as flats and to the right of the white key are known as sharps. So, you have "B Sharp" or "B Flat," for example.

An easy way to remember this is to think about how your cutlery is laid out on the table. Your knife is sharp and always laid out to the right of your plate. That makes it easy to remember that right is sharp.

Now, because the black keys have a white key on either side of them, they can be called sharps or flats interchangeably. If you look to the right of a white "B" key on your keyboard, the black key is "C Sharp." But it is also left of the white "D" key and so is "D Flat." Don't overthink it too much – it is not all that important right now, and we go into it in more detail in Chapter 6 anyway.

What is more important is to learn your way around the keyboard – think more in terms of the letter, rather than it being a sharp or flat.

Quick Exercise: Now you know how to find your "C" and "F" notes and, because of this, how to find the others as well. Play each "C" note on the black and white keys and listen to how each sounds. Do the same for all the other keys as well.

Now try something a little more complicated. Position your thumb over any white key and your forefinger over the corresponding black key. Play each in quick succession. Then try playing them together. Experiment a little until you find the tones that match one another more closely.

Intervals

These are the distance between the different notes. A semitone, or half-step, will always separate the black key from the white key next to is. Where the white keys are not broken by black keys, like between "B" and "C" or "E" and "F", the difference in the note is a semitone.

A full tone is the space between two white keys that have a black key in between them, like "C" and "D".

Chapter Summary

- Your keyboard is made up of 52 white keys and 36 black keys. (Some older keyboards have fewer keys.)
- Each key represents a particular musical note.
- There are seven musical notes that we use in music – these are named A through to G.
- The black keys are grouped in twins or triplets to help you locate the different notes more easily.
- The white key to the left of a twin is always "C." The white key to the left of a triplet is always an "F."

- To remember the difference, remember that "C" has two points to it and "F" has three to it.
- The black keys take their names from the white keys closest to them.
- The black key to the right of a white key is called sharp. The one to the left of a white key is called flat.
- An easy way to remember this is that knives are sharp and are always put to the right of your plate when the table is laid.
- Intervals refer to the difference in sound between the white and black keys.

In the next chapter, you will learn about the pedals on your piano and how to use them.

Chapter Two: The Pedals

In this chapter, you will learn how and when to use the pedals on your piano. This is the second step in our seven-point plan in helping you learn to play the piano.

The pedals on the piano are not just there for decoration. You use the pedals for sounds that are not possible using just your hands. Most standard pianos will have two such foot pedals – the Una Corda on the left and the Sustain on the right. Some pianos have three pedals. The extra pedal in the middle is called the Sostenuto, but it is seldom used.

The Una Corda Pedal (The Soft Pedal)

Use your left foot to play this pedal. It helps to soften notes, so could be used when you are first starting to build up to a crescendo. It will not work on very loud notes, so the range is limited somewhat.

The Sustain Pedal

You will use your right foot with this pedal. It elongates your note's sound and causes it to resonate after you have lifted your fingers from the key. The resonance will be held until you take your foot off the pedal. This is usually used to bridge harmonies. With this pedal, as long as you are pressing the pedal, all the notes you play will be sustained.

The Sostenuto

As mentioned before, this is not something that you will use very often. You would normally use your right foot to play it, and it is similar to the Sustain Pedal in that it sustains the notes played. The difference between this pedal and the previous one is that the Sostenuto pedal only sustains the notes that you were playing when you pressed the pedals. Any notes played after that will play as normal.

Using the Pedals

When you start playing, get into position and position the balls of your feet above the pedals. Your heels should still touch the ground; this will help you maintain a good posture and also allow you to keep a light touch when it comes to depressing the pedals.

What you need to keep in mind is that this is not a stomping contest. You need to practice lifting your foot off the pedals gently. If you take your foot off too quickly, it can create a noisy bang; It can take a little practice to get used to using the pedals smoothly. Just think of it like parking your car – you don't smash the accelerator to the ground when parking, you ease into the parking slowly.

If the music calls for the use of the pedal, you will see the word "Ped" marked where you need to apply the pedal. Alternatively, the composition may call for the use of it all the way through the piece. You can release the pedal when you see an asterisk on the sheet. This will look like:

Quick exercise: Try using the pedals in conjunction with the lines of "It's Raining it's Pouring" that you learned in the previous chapter. Mix it up a little, play the same tune using the Una Corda pedal from time to time and then listen to how it sounds when you use the Sustain pedal instead. If you do have a Sostenuto panel, play around with that one as well.

Chapter Summary

- Most pianos have two pedals – the Una Corda pedal and the Sustain pedal.
- Some pianos have a third pedal – the Sostenuto pedal.

- The Una Corda pedal is always on the left; the Sustain pedal is always on the right. If the Sostenuto pedal is there, it will be in the middle.
- You will not use the Sostenuto pedal very often.
- The Una Corda pedal helps to soften notes.
- The Sustain pedal keeps the notes going for as long as you have the pedal down. It will do this for all notes played, while the pedal is down.
- The Sostenuto pedal isolates the note that was played when the pedal was first pressed and sustains only that particular note. The rest are played as normal.

In the next chapter, you will learn how to read some basic sheet music for yourself.

Chapter Three: Reading Sheet Music

In this chapter, you will learn what many of those dots and lines mean when it comes to sheet music. This is the third quick step in the program.

You need to know something about reading music in order to progress. Think of sheet music like a script for a movie, except that it is written using musical symbols rather than words. The composer could, technically, write out the words but it would make playing the music much slower and difficult because you would have to read each word.

Symbols are a lot easier to read, once you understand what they mean. The composer tells you which notes you should play, when to pause, how long to pause for, and even the pace at which you should play.

A sheet of music will look something like this:

Everything You Need to Know About a Piano Score

If you look at the score above, you will see a lot of dots, dashes, and other symbols. It looks a little confusing, but it's not so bad if you take it a note at a time. Each of the notes tells you which key you need to play and how long you need to play it for.

To keep the notes in some semblance of order, they are written on a five-line stave.

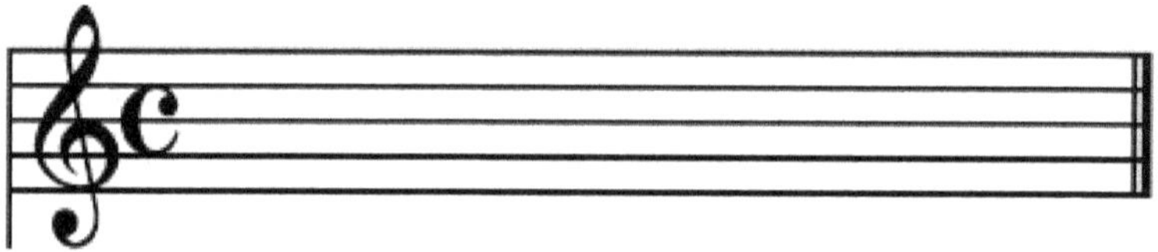

Starting with the Stave

The notes can be placed on the lines, or in the spaces between lines. Each line or space represents a specific note. The notes are divided up into equal sections called measured. These are separated from one another by bar lines – vertical lines at the end of that particular measure. The stave will normally start with some type of clef (The stylized "G" in the illustration above), and this may be followed by a sharp or a flat (The "C" in the illustration above.)

In addition, the markings above the stave will usually tell you what speed to play at. The markings underneath the stave will tell you what volume that section is to be played at.

You will see that there are usually two staves joined together with brackets, with different symbols at the top and bottom. This is known as a grand stave. It is denoted like this because you need to play both staves together – one set being the notes to play with your right hand, the other the notes to play with your left hand.

Don't worry about this too much at this stage – the main tune is usually shown in the stave for the right hand, so you don't need to pay attention to both now. In fact, as you will see later, you don't even have to have these two to play a tune so if you find it confusing, don't stress about it. We have a way around that.

The Basic Symbols to Learn

The Treble Clef

This is the stylized G that we were talking about in the previous section. There are a number of different ways that this is written. The treble clef shown below will denote which keys you need to play with your left hand. X

The treble clef looks like:

The Base Clef

This shows the part of the music to be played with your left hand. (To start out with, we are not going to worry too much about the left-hand section.) The base clef looks like:

The Key Signature

This is another thing that might appear at the start of the music. It shows which of the notes need to be played as flats and which need to be played as sharps.

This is what this will look like on your sheet music:

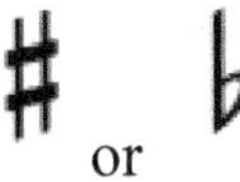

The Time Signature

This can be any two numbers. The numbers tell you how many beats there are in each measure. (We go over this in more detail in Chapter Seven.) This will look like:

$$\frac{2}{2}$$

Tempo Marking

This is a way of showing you what tempo the piece should be played at. The notation below shows the number of crotchet beats to play in a minute. Alternatively, they could write out what speed the piece is to be played at. This will often be in Italian like "Presto". (We go over each of these in more detail in Chapter 7).

This will look like:

$=130$

Dynamics

This lets you know what volume you need to play at. The "P" in the above diagram means Piano, or quiet. The "F" in the above means Forte or loudly. If the symbol has an "M" after it, it means moderate volume. (We are not really going to worry too much about that in these lessons though.) These symbols look like:

$$p$$

$$f$$

The Notes

These relate to the actual notes that you are playing so let's go into them in a little more detail. A note is generally made up of a head (the dot) and a stem, the vertical line that is either above or below the dot. Your notes will look something like:

Whole Notes

This is a whole note and will be one of the only ones that doesn't have a vertical line. This is meant to last four beats.

Half Notes

These are half notes or minimums and are played for two beats. You can tell that they are half notes because the dot is not filled in.

Quarter Notes

These are quarter notes – you will normally play four of these in one measure. (More about that in Chapter Seven).

Quavers and Semi-Quavers

These are eighth notes or quavers and sixteen notes or semiquavers.

Where the Notes Are Displayed

There are two shortcuts that you can use to remember which line or space each note is displayed in. Remember how we said that some of the notes are displayed on the lines, and some are displayed in the spaces in between them, this is how you remember what notes go where.

For The Lines

Remember the mnemonic device, Every Good Boy Deserves Fruit. In this case, the "E" note is recorded on the top line, the "G" note on the next line down, the "B" note on the middle line, the "D" note on the next line down and the "F" note on the final line.

For The Spaces

Remember the word FACE to keep this one straight but this time start from the space at the bottom and work your way up. So, the "F" note is in the final space of the stave, the "A" note is in the next space up, the "C" note is in the space second from the top, and the "E" note is in the space right at the top of the stave. In this case, the "F" note is an octave lower than in the previous example.

A Quick Shortcut

I am now going to teach you a shortcut to playing popular music. This only works with music that has words to it, but it is a great shortcut and is more than enough if you just want to be able to play some tunes for the family.

The sheet music example we displayed previously was made up of grand staves. When you have lyrics as well, these are displayed in the vocal line. This is a stave that is directly above the grand staves and is a much more simplified version of the notes. It will usually have a treble stave at the very front.

If you want to start playing music quickly and easily, concentrate on the vocal line only. This allows you to play at the pace that suits you and is a lot easier than having to read the more complex staves beneath it.

The additional advantage of doing this is that you can buy music sheets that only have the vocal line on them. If your main aim is to be able to play a few tunes, this can save you a lot of money and space because the grand staves are not usually included in these copies.

Quick Exercise: Go to http://www.music-for-music-teachers.com/silent-night-sheet-music.html, and you can download the sheet music for "Silent Night" for free, in a simple format. It's a fairly simple composition and one that you probably already know the melody for. See how well you can follow along on your piano.

Chapter Summary

- You need to know what the different symbols on sheet music are in order to be able to interpret it.

- Sheet music is set out in a five-line stave. You can see which note to play based on where it is placed in the stave and also the symbol used.
- Things like the general tempo of the piece will be listed at the beginning of the stave.
- Notations above and below the stave can show the speed at which a piece is to be played and what volume to play it at.
- A stave will usually consist of at least two separate sections, one for the notes to be played with the left hand and one for the notes to be played with the right hand. These two staves should be played at the same time and so are bracketed together to form a grand stave. (We are not going to do that right now, though.)
- The symbol for the note will tell you what note to play and how long to play it for.
- Each note is displayed on a different line, or space, in the stave.
- An easy way to remember which note goes on which line is to remember "Every Boy Deserves Good Fruit." This is read from the top line to the bottom one.
- An easy way to remember which note goes into what space, is to remember the word "FACE." In this case, the spaces are read from the bottom up. The notes used in this case are an octave lower than in the previous instance.
- To make things a lot easier for yourself, you can read the music from the vocal line. This is a much more simplified stave meant to be read by singers so

it does not have all the symbols a grand stave would
have and does not have them separated into notes to
be played by the left hand and notes to be played by
the right hand.

In the next chapter, you will learn about more about
practicing scales and why it is not a boring time waster.

Chapter Four: Practising Scales

In this chapter, you will learn about scales and why you should look forward to practicing them. This is your fourth lesson – you are almost there now.

Now that you understand about which keys are which, know when to use the pedals and know something about reading sheet music, we are ready to move on to playing scales. This is the fourth step in our program.

How did you do with playing "Silent Night?" It should have been relatively simple for you – you might have made a mistake or two here or there, but, overall, you should have been able to follow it. See how easy it is to start playing real music? And you can play popular songs like that without ever having to worry about learning scales.

However, there is a good reason that one of the first things you normally learn to play on a piano are scales. Now, admittedly, this can seem a little boring, but it is good practice. Scales are a great way for you to build up a working knowledge of the melodies in a song and to also give your fingers more practice. So, while you can play without practicing scales, if you really want to start getting better, you will have to spend some time on this.

The most important thing about scales is that you should repeat them over and over again. Think of it like a putting green in golf – you are there to practice your swing, not to actually play a game. The more you practice, however, the better your swing gets and the better you are able to play when you actually head out to the course. The same applies for practicing scales on your piano.

What is a Scale?

It is a series of notes that follow on from one another in a particular order. The most commonly encountered scales are major scales and minor scales. They both have the following commonalities:

- They are both eight notes in length.
- The topmost note and the bottommost note are only an octave apart.
- Each note is done in order from lowest to highest or highest to lowest. You do not mix up the order of the notes at all.
- Scales are made up of a combination of half- or whole steps.

If you understand how the scales work, you are able to build any type of scale you want, just by adding in the right sequence of steps. Scales form the basis for creating chords and allowing you to learn to improvise. You will need to know these if you want to start composing your own music.

The scales that you choose to practice will be dependent on what musical style you are most interested in. It is, however, a good idea to start by learning the major scales and then move on to practicing the minor scales.

Major Scales

The pattern here will be a tone, a tone, a semitone, a tone, atone, a tone, and a semitone. It is pretty easy to work out, as long as you start on the right note. All major scales will be based on the same principle.

You can, for example, play an "C" scale in major. You can start on "C" and then move up through the other notes, using only the white keys. The "C" major scale is one of the easiest to start with because you only need to concentrate on the white keys.

Major scales are generally thought to be livelier in nature.

Minor Scales

Once you are more comfortable with major scales, you can try your hand at minor scales. The minor scales are available in three separate versions – the harmonic or the natural or the melodic scales. What this means is that every minor scale has three separate formats to learn.

The Natural Minor Scales

This is the key minor scale to practice. The difference between it and your major scale is that you start with the A note and then finish off again with the A note.

The Harmonic Minor Scales

This also follows a set pattern, but it is slightly different. It is a tone, a semitone, a tone, a tone, a semitone, a tone + a half and a semitone. This pattern is often described as a bit eerie in nature and will lend something of a haunting quality to your work.

The Melodic Minor Scales

This is more complex because you will use the pattern, a tone, a tone, a semitone, atone, a tone, a semitone and then a tone when working your way up the scales. When working your way back, it changes to a tone, a tone, a semitone, a tone, a tone, a semitone, and finishes on tone.

What makes this scale useful, is that it teaches you to be more flexible when it comes to your other scales. When practicing your minor scales, it is best to start with the A minor scales because these are easiest.

Quick Exercise: Practice this now - find the Middle C and practice working your way through all seven notes. You would start by using your thumb and the rest of the fingers on your right hand and then bring in your left hand for the final two keys. Practice this working your way up the scales, and then down them again.

When you have mastered that, you can move on to practicing more scales. You can try starting with a different note, always remembering to move up either half a step or a whole step. Here is an illustration of the different C Scales that you can use to get you started with your practicing.

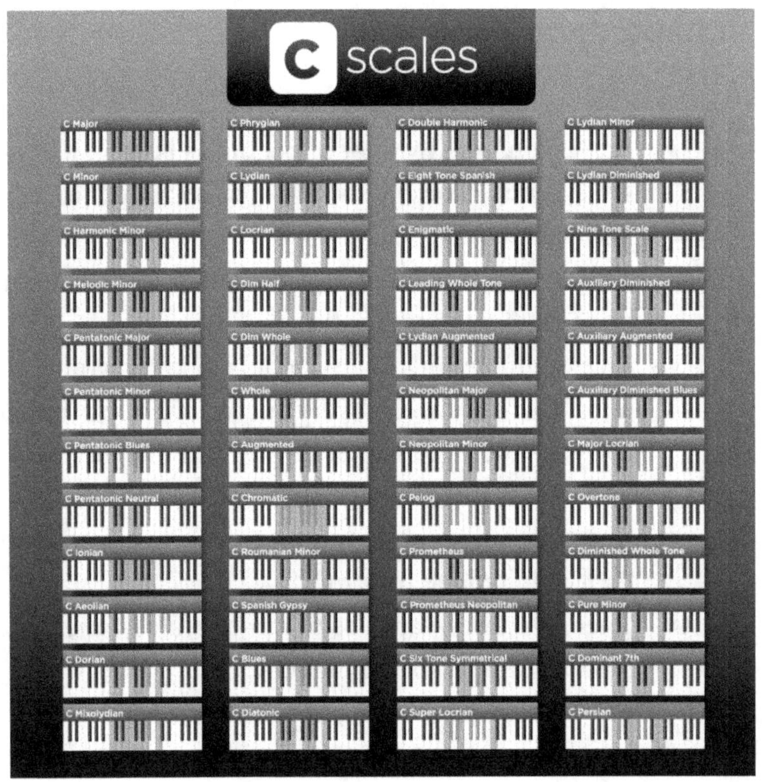

Most of the C scales shown above can be accomplished using your right hand only. It is also important to practice scales using your left hand, so don't just focus on one type. Try to practice at least three different scales a day for at least ten minutes overall in order to get better at them.

Chapter Summary

- Scales are seen by a lot of people as boring, but they are essential exercises when it comes to getting to know the keys.
- They can also be used as warmups or to help build up the strength in your finger.
- The key to getting scales right is to know your intervals really well. Every successive key is either a half- or whole step up or down from the previous one.
- There are minor scales and major scales, each with their own unique pattern.
- There are three varieties of minor scales – the natural, harmonic and melodic.

In the next chapter, you will learn about using chords to make the melodies sound richer.

Chapter Five: Adding in Chords

In this chapter, you will learn about adding in chords. This is the fifth step in the program.

Chords are important in creating harmonies. You will distinguish them on your music sheet because they will have three or four notes stacked on top of one another.

What is a Chord?

A chord is made up of at least three tones, played simultaneously, where the intervals are based on a set formula. So, slamming your fingers down on four or five random keys may be fun, but is not a chord.

Three-Note Chords

These are the simplest ones to work with and are also known as triads. You will normally play these by using your pinky, thumb, and forefinger. Chords begin very simply. Like melodies, chords are based on scales.

Chords are essentially based on scales, the difference being that with scales, each note is played in succession. With chords, all of the notes are played together.

The root note is the note that you start with. The chord will be named for this note. If you are using a basic triad, you will have your root note and two other notes, notes that are at a third interval from the first note and at the fifth interval from the first note.

You can add to the chord by moving up a step or a half-step, or by adding extra notes in. To make things easier for you, though, I have included a list of all the basic chords at the end of this chapter.

Major Chords

These are the ones that you will use most often and are the easiest to play. A lot of the songs that you play, including Silent Night, consist of major chords. Major chords are based on your major scales. The first example in the illustration below is an example of a major chord.

Most of the time, composers will omit writing "Major" when using a chord. They simply use the symbol for chord above the staff of it to show which chord it is. If you see the symbol for a chord, and nothing naming it, you can assume that it is a major chord.

Other Chords You May Encounter

You are mostly going to be dealing with major or minor chords, but that does not mean that these are all that there is.

Other chords are formed by adding extra notes to your standard major or minor chord.

Augmented Chords And Diminished Chords

The only real difference in a major or minor chord is the third interval. The fifth interval, however, is always the same and it is here that you can play around to create a new chord altogether.

Augmented chords consist of the root note, your major third interval, and an augmented fifth interval. With augmented chords, you raise the final note by another half-step and always work with a major chord to start with. Here are examples of augmented chords.

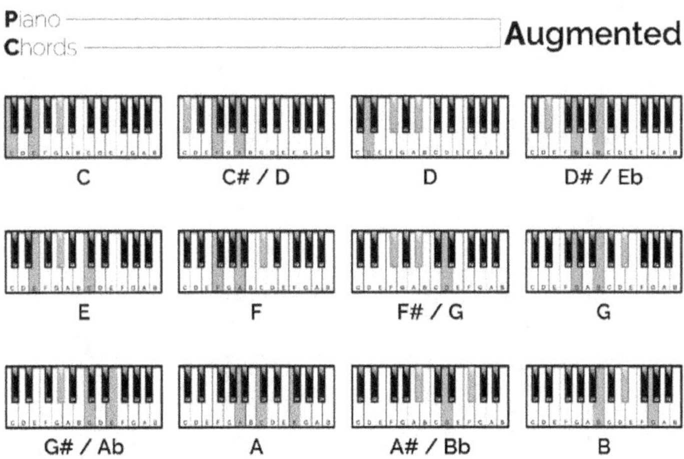

Diminished chords consist of the root note, your minor third interval, and your diminished fifth interval. In this case, you lower the final note by half a step and always work with a minor chord to start with. You would normally see them with "Dim" in the name.

Here are some examples of diminished chords:

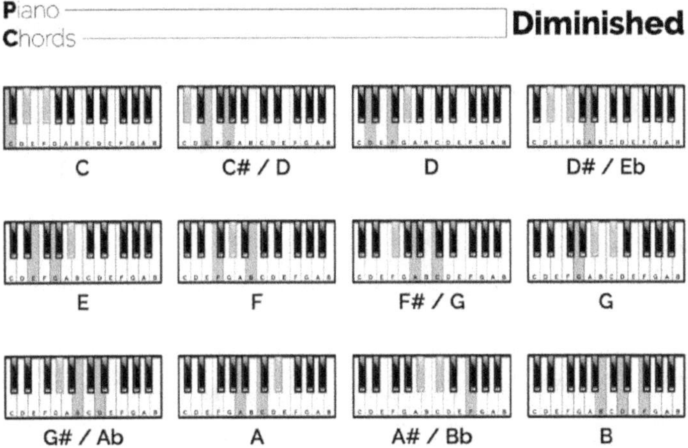

Suspended Chords

This is considered a three-note chord, but it is not really a triad. In this case, one of the notes is left hanging, meaning that you need to wait for the next one. There are two options when it comes to suspended chords – The second and fourth suspended chords. They will have "Sus" in the name.

A suspended two chord is made up of the root note, the major second interval, and the fifth interval. A suspended four chord is made up of the root note, the fourth interval, and the fifth interval.

Generally speaking, a suspended chord will usually be followed by another note, but they can also be used on their own.

Here are examples of suspended chords:

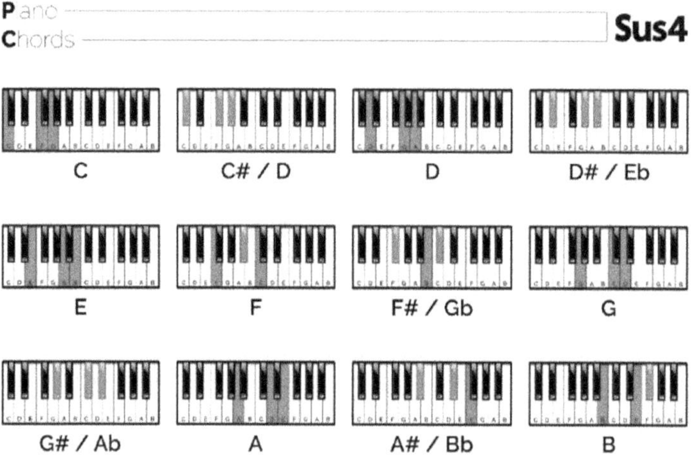

Adding a Seventh Interval

A triad is a basic kind of chord. In order to make it more interesting, you can add other notes at the end in the form of a seventh interval. It is usually used in a composition to help create suspense and will usually be followed by a major chord or minor chord. On its own, it is not likely to sound great, but when added to a triad, it improves the sound.

You can choose to add any of the chords we have discussed here to create this seventh interval.

The Chord Symbols

Chord symbols let you know the type of chord and what the root note of the chord is. These will start with the letter of the root note. (Keep in mind that with a major chord, this will be all there is.)

With other chords, you will have either a letter in the name, such as "M" to indicate a minor chord and/ or a letter like "7" to indicate the seventh chord. So, if, for example, you see the name Dm6, you know you have that you are playing the D minor chord with a sixth interval.

The chord is played along with the note that is shown underneath it. You will hold this chord until you see a new chord symbol or change of cord marked in the music.

Chord Inversions

It's not the most interesting exercise to play the same chords over and over again. You really don't need to do this at all. It doesn't matter what you do with the basic chords; they will always sound exactly the same.

That is where chord inversions come into play. They allow you to change up the sound of a chord. So instead of playing the root chord, and following it with the third chord and fifth chord, as usual, you could change things up by starting with the final chord and ending on the root chord. So now what you are doing is to play the root chord an octave higher than the standard chords.

Inversions can also help you to transition from one chord to the next. Let's say you are playing a C major chord, followed by an A minor chord. This would mean playing the C chord and then moving your hand over to play the next set of keys – it would be somewhat clumsy.

If you use an inversion, though, your hand will end up in the correct position as you end off the C chord, allowing you to play with a lot less effort.

Using Chord Progressions

Chord progression means moving through a range of chords in the same key signature. Imagine how boring it would be if you played the same chord throughout the entire piece. You can use chord progressions to liven things up a bit or to move from one signature to the next.

Arpeggios

You don't always have to play the notes that make up your chord at the same time. You can also rather play them one after another in sequence. Arpeggios help to keep the piece moving. You would, for example, instead of playing a typical C major chord, play each note, starting with the "C," individually. You would then play the "C" in the next octave before reversing the order of play and going back down to the first "C" you played.

This would just be one possible version so try changing it up a bit. This is also possible using minor chords – you just would not need to descend at the end of the structure again.

A Round-Up of Different Chords That You Might Come Across

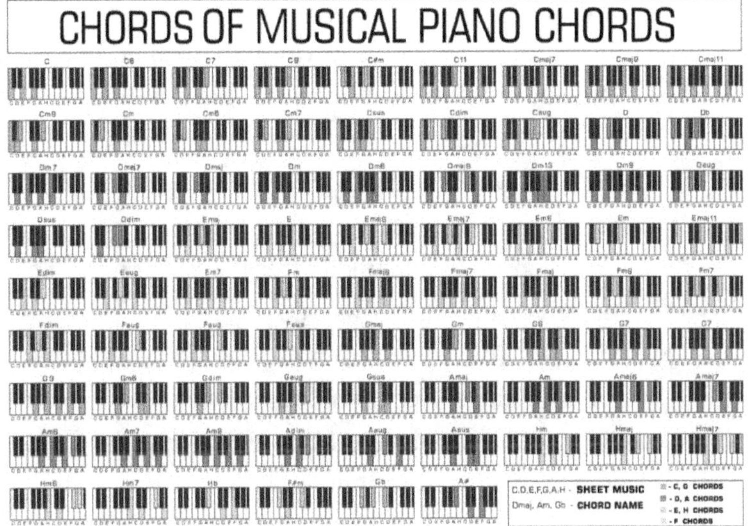

Chapter Summary

- Chords are notes that are played together to create a more harmonious composition.
- On the music sheet, a chord is denoted if there are three notes stacked together.

- Chords are at least three notes long and are calculated according to set formulae rather than just being chosen at random.
- A chord is usually based on the scales that you use.
- There are many different kinds of chords.
- Augmented chords are created from major scales and have the last note going up by half a step.
- Diminished chords are created from minor scales and have the last note dropping by half a step. They will have "Dim" in their name.
- Suspended chords leave you hanging and need to be finished off with another note. They will have "Sus" in their name.
- You can add another interval in order to make the chord more interesting.
- Major chords are named after their root note. So, a C major cord is simply named "C."
- You can invert cords to make them more interesting and to make the play smoother. This means starting with your top note and carrying on into the next octave with your root note.
- Chord progressions can make the piece more interesting and can help bridge one signature line with another.
- Arpeggios are another way to change things up – you play exactly the same notes, except this time you change things up by playing the notes in sequence rather than together.

In the next chapter, you will learn more about sharps and flats.

Chapter Six: Sharps and Flats

In this chapter, you will learn how to start incorporating the black keys and how to recognize when to do so. This is your sixth lesson.

The symbols that we deal with in this chapter are also known as accidentals. These "accidentals" tell you when to use the black keys, or how to modify your note's pitch.

As mentioned previously, the black keys are called sharps or flats, and named for the white keys directly next to them. Let's do a quick recap. If the black key is to the right of the white key, it will be that key's sharp. If it is to the left of that key, it will be that key's flat.

Here's a diagram of how this would look on your actual keyboard:

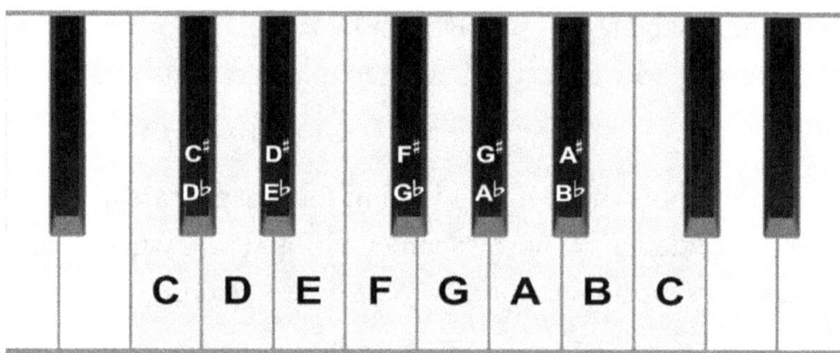

On the sheet music, you will see the symbol for the sharp or the flat directly before the note, next to the head of the note that it applies to.

Sharps

Sharps raise the pitch by a half-step or semitone. The symbol for a sharp is:

Flats

Flats lower the pitch by a half-step or semitone. The symbol for a flat is:

♭

The Natural Key

This tells you that it is time to stop using the black keys. It will precede the natural note and tell you that you should play all the remaining notes in that series as natural notes. The symbol for the natural key is:

♮

The Key Signature

You will also see these notes directly after the clef or base staves and before any time signature. This is what is referred to as the key signature, and it lets you know what key to use for the tune, and how many sharps and flats there are in the piece. You will need to look this over before starting.

Once you have been practicing your scales, this gets a whole lot simpler to do. All of the keys except for A minor and C major have both flats and sharps.

Chapter Summary

- Accidentals are used to change the pitch of notes – they change the pitch by a half-tone or semitone.
- The three accidentals are Flat, Sharp and Natural.
- To get the flat and sharp notes, you have to use the black keys on the keyboard.
- The flat takes its name from the white key to its left and reduces the pitch.
- The sharp takes its name from the black key to its right and increases the pitch.
- So, every black key is both a sharp and a flat.
- The natural symbol tells you to revert to stop using the black keys.

In the next chapter, you will learn why timing is so important and how you can get this critical aspect right.

Chapter Seven: It's All About the Timing

In this chapter, you will learn the final and possibly most important element in this book – how to get the timing right. This is the final step in our program.

There is more to music than getting the notes and chords right. (Sure, that is obviously a big piece of the puzzle, but you also need to be able to get the timing and beat right.) In fact, you might be able to slip an incorrect chord or note past your audience without them noticing, but they will notice immediately if your timing is off.

The timing of the notes is what makes the music happy or sad. If we never adjusted the tempo at which we played, every piece of music would sound pretty much the same. Each note has a point where it starts and a point where it ends. As a result, we need to assign values to this length that we are able to count. In this chapter, we are going to learn how to really get the rhythm going and keep it going.

The Beat

When you are listening to music and clapping along or tapping your foot in time with it, the beat is what you are trying to keep up with. The faster the beat, the faster and more energetic the song. The slower the beat, the slower the music is. Getting the tempo, or how fast the beat is, right is extremely important.

Use Tempo to Measure the Beat

When it comes to music, time gets measured in beats. In this case, the number of beats per minute. If you want a piece to sound correct, you need to pay attention to the beat.

Quick Exercise: Get out your smartphone and set the timer for a minute. Every two seconds, tap your foot once. That's a beat. Now, you can speed this up by increasing the number of taps to one per second, or slow it down to one tap every three seconds. That's the tempo.

In the exercise above, the first beat was 30 beats per minute because you tapped your foot 30 times. The second beat was 20 beats per minute because you slowed it down. In both cases, the beat was steady because you were timing your taps to the second.

When reading music, you would refer to the tempo marking to tell you what speed to play the music at. This will either be in the form of either a written word to tell you what pace to use, or a metronome marking that will tell you exactly how many beats per minute.

You can follow the guidelines in the table below to see what the basic readings are in terms of tempo.

Written	Translation	Number of Beats Per Minute
Largo	Very Slow	40 – 60
Adagio	Slow	61 - 72
Andante	Moderate	73 – 96
Allegro	Fast	97 - 132
Vivace	Faster	133 – 168
Presto	Very Fast	169 - 208

Measuring Tempo

When you are playing a piece of music, you won't be able to check your smartphone to see how many seconds have elapsed. A metronome is a handy device that can help you instead. You set it to the rate that you like, and it will tick out the rhythm accordingly.

The Grouping of Beats

Remember how I said earlier that the sheet of music was like a script? Every note is recorded in the order that it is meant to be played in. Unlike a script, however, the stave can be divided up into equal sections of time. These smaller sections make it possible to check the beat and to understand whereabouts you are in the actual composition.

Now, in a slower tempo song, this might not be much of a problem, but when it comes to faster-paced music, you could have a few hundred different beats in just a few minutes. Keeping track of the beat in this manner would mean counting high numbers when you are trying to concentrate on what you are doing.

It would become difficult to do this, so composers have come up with a workaround. Instead, the music is divided up into measures – smaller bits that are easier to keep track of. The number of beats in a measure will normally be decided by the composer, and this can change. They will indicate the end of a measure by drawing a vertical line, or bar line, through all the lines and spaces of the stave. This will look something like:

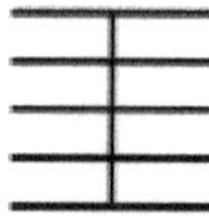

Most compositions, however, will have four beats per measure. This means that you would just have to count to four each time when playing – not too difficult a task. The measures break the music into segments or patterns that we can then use to help determine the time signature of the piece.

The Rhythm of Melody

Without the melody of notes played, the beat wouldn't mean much at all. The different lengths of the notes are what makes the music more interesting. It's like listening to a good public speaker – they change the cadence of their voice and mix up the tones so that it sounds more interesting.

In contrast, if the speaker just spoke in a monotone, without varying the tone or rhythm, it wouldn't be long before everyone became bored with the speech. The same is true of music.

Some music is very distinctive – you can recognize the tune just by hearing the beat. Take "Jingle Bells" for example – you don't have to hear it being played on an instrument to recognize it, you could tap out the beat with your foot, and someone would still recognize it.

We said earlier that you could get away with not having to read all the characters on a standard music sheet. You do, however, need to know exactly how much time every note is meant to last for. At the beginning of the piece, the composer lets you know how many equal pieces to divide each measure into. That means working out fractions but, in this case, it's not hard.

Think of it like cutting up a pizza. You can divide the pizza up into halves, quarters or eighths, or more if you like. When it comes to music, this usually translates into four pieces of "pizza" per measure. Or, more accurately, four quarter notes, or four beats. This is represented by the most common music symbol:

You will always know if a note is a quarter note because the head will always be completely black. In our example, you have divided the pizza up into four equal slices and are eating just one, so it is finished faster. In the same way, the notes are played faster and not held for as long.

Quick Exercise: Set your metronome to one beat per second. Every time it clicks, play one-quarter note in whichever key you prefer. Stick to a single note, for now, say for example, "C" so that you can get the hang of playing to the beat. Every time the metronome clicks, hit the "C" key. Get this right before moving on to the next section.

Half Notes

Alternatively, you could choose to divide the pizza into halves and eat one piece again. You will take longer to eat the pizza because there is more of it. By a similar token, half notes are longer than quarter notes, so you would divide the measure up into two instead of four. So, it would now be two beats per measure instead of just one.

This would be represented on the sheet as follows:

Quick Exercise: Set your metronome to one beat per second again, and this time, play a note on every second click. You would hold the key down for the count of these two beats.

Why do the Stems Get Displayed Differently?

You will notice in the examples above, that there are two ways to show the stem of a note – either pointing up or pointing down. Why is that? Any notes that are either on the middle line of the stave or above it, will have their stems underneath the note head and to the right. Any notes that fall below this will have the stems above the note head and to the left.

This helps to make a clearer distinction between the notes on different lines. If all the notes were just circles, it would be a lot harder to keep your place when reading the music quickly.

Whole Notes

A whole note lasts the entire measure for a count of four. So, back to our pizza example, if you ate the whole thing, it would take longer.

It is a simple circle and looks like this:

O

Playing a whole note is pretty simple, just count to four and then play the note. You would just need to make sure that the note lasts for the length of the measure.

Quick Exercise: Set your metronome to one beat per second and again, hold down any key you like. Hold it down for the count of four clicks and then move on to play the next note.

Putting It All Together

Now that you know how the count works, and know how long to hold the keys down for and what the basic note values are, you can start playing around a little and we can move onto the more complex notes.

Again, if you were only to stick to full, half and quarter notes, there would only be so much variation that you would be able to achieve. You can divide it up even more to fit in more notes per measure and increase the tempo.

You don't actually change the speed, but you are holding the notes down for smaller periods at a time. It may take some getting used to so, if you are battling, to keep up, slow things down a bit by slowing the speed of your playing.As you get more used to this rate, and more familiar with the eighth notes, and sixteenth notes, you can start to speed up again.

Eighth Notes

Eighth notes are also known as quavers.This is like your pizza into eight pieces. To eat a piece won't take as long as it would if you were eating half the pizza because you are getting much less pizza. By the same token, you just need to hold the note down for a lot less time, and move faster through the notes in the same measure. Instead of fitting 4-beats into a measure, you need to fit in eight so you will need to speed up your metronome. The symbol for an eighth note is:

If there are two or more of these notes, the flag changes to a solid beam and connects the notes. This helps in making the beat a lot more obvious. It will look something like this:

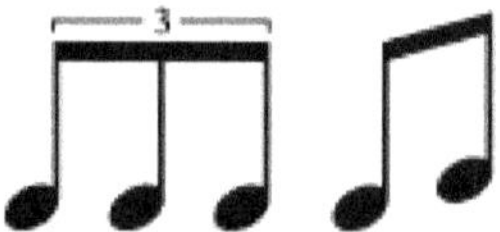

Sixteenth Notes

Sixteenth notes are also known as semi-quavers. The same rule applies to sixteenth notes. Like with eighth notes, when they are by single notes, they are shown with flags – except this time there are two flags.

When there are more than one of these in a row, the flags are changed to beams, as follows:

It is quite common to see four such notes placed together in this way because that represents one beat. You might also find it joined with an eighth note as follows:

Now, if you can slow things down a lot, it is pretty easy to play these notes. However, if you play them at the tempo that they are meant to be played at, it starts getting more complicated. That said, with practice, you will be fine to play these notes as well.

And dividing up the beat doesn't stop at sixteenths, some composers go a step further and halve it again so that it is 32nds, 64ths or 128ths. They show this in the composition by increasing the number of flags. I am not going to go into examples here because these are not as common as the eighth notes and sixteenth notes and should be left until you have had a bit more practice.

Rests

No matter how much practice you have, there is only a certain amount that you will be able to do. Your fingers are going to need a break from time to time and so will your audience. These breaks can be quick or a little longer, but the defining character of them is that you are not playing anything. You continue to count the beat, but you don't actually play or hold any kind of note.

In orchestral compositions, this will often be where the strings take over or someone playing another instrument gets their own solo. All you need to do is to relax your hands and keep them poised over the keys and make sure that you keep up with the count. Just like there are different note lengths, there are different rest periods. Let's have a look at these.

Whole And Half Rests

Let's say that you are playing a whole "C". You press the key and keep it depressed for a count of four beats. When you are playing half note, you keep it down for half as long. Rests will work in a similar fashion – you won't play anymore for the same number of beats.

I like to think of the symbol for the whole rest as a comfortable bed that you can sink into. You would relax for a decent period. It will always be on the fourth line or above so that it is easier to spot. It looks like this:

The half rest is the same symbol, turned upside down. So, still a bed but a little less comfortable. It will always sit on the middle line. It looks like this:

Quarter Rests and Beyond

These are the same as your quarter, eighth and sixteenth notes in terms of timing. Here are the symbols – from left to right, these are the symbols for the quarter, eighth and sixteenth rest respectively.

Time Signatures

In music, a time signature is what you use to find out the meter of the piece. The time signature is split into two numbers; the top number number tells you the meter of the piece you're playing. So, if the number is 4 over 4, that means there are four quarter note beats. If it is 2 over 2, there are two half note beats.

If the composer wants to use more than one type of note, like one-half note and two-quarter notes, that is fine – they could show this as 2 over 4 and 1 over 2. They do need to ensure that the top number adds up to a whole number in the end. So, one-half note and two-quarter notes, if we add them mathematically, would total 4 quarters in total and this makes sense.

If the composer tried to say three-quarter notes and one-half note, you would end up with too many beats, and this would not work. So, you should never see a time signature that is something like 5 over 4.

Common Time

Most composers stick to common time, i.e., 4 over 4. They indicate this by using the letter "C" in place of the standard time signature. It will appear directly after the clef symbol of the stave. This is how this would be displayed within the stave:

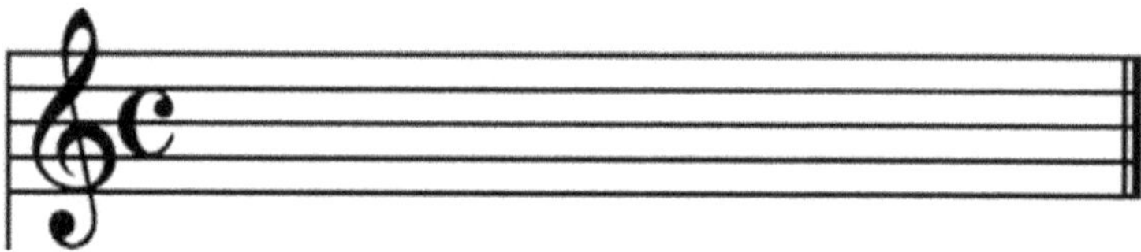

Chapter Summary

- The beat needs to be measured and kept at a steady pace.
- The faster the tempo that the notes are played at, the more energetic the pace of the piece.
- Beats are grouped in measures. These break up the music into equal sections. The composer will decide how many beats to use per measure.
- A whole note will take up a full measure, or four full beats. So, you would hold the note for the full length of that measure and only press the note once during that particular measure.
- A half note is half as long so there will be two beats in one measure.

- The notes can be divided into quarters, eighths and sixteenths as well. Each of these is shorter than the last so there will be more notes to play within each measure. This means that as the tempo increases the smaller the notes get.

- If you are still learning, slow down the tempo until you get used to playing the notes in the right succession. Then you can start worrying about speeding up again.

- The stems of the notes are arbitrary, used more as a way of differentiating the notes than having a very specific meaning.

- Rests are just as important when it comes to playing – they give you time to have a break and also give your audience a little break as well.

- A rest is usually similar in length to the note preceding it. The main thing to remember is to keep track of the beat.

- During a rest, keep your hands relaxed but poised at the ready for the next lot of notes.

Final Words

Well done – you have completed the program. Learning to play the piano can be fun, and it really is not that hard once you know the basics. It's a simple seven-step process:

- Step One: Learn the Keyboard and the keys.
- Step Two: Learn how and when to use the pedals.
- Step Three: Learn something about reading sheet music.
- Step Four: Practice your scales.
- Step Five: Learn about adding chords.
- Step Six: Learn when to use sharps and flats.
- Step Seven: Learn to get the tempo right.

In this book, we have started you off on the basics you need to play your first full composition. You should now be able to play some simple tunes and impress your friends with how fast your learned this skill.

From now forward, all it takes to really master the piano is to practice, and you get to decide how far you want to go. You can choose to practice every day, or trot your skills out on high days and holidays – it really is completely up to you.

Image Credit: Shutterstock.com

MUSIC
THEORY
FOR BEGINNERS
The Only 7 Exercises You Need to Learn
Music Fundamentals and the Elements
of Written Music Today
PRESTON HOFFMAN

BOOK 2

MUSIC THEORY: FOR BEGINNERS

The Only 7 Exercises You Need to Learn Music Fundamentals and the Elements of Written Music Today

Preston Hoffman

Table of Contents

Introduction.. 73

Chapter One: Understanding Music Theory............................ 75

Chapter Two: Learning the Staff................................. 82

Chapter Three: Understanding Common Notation 88

Chapter Four: The Basic Elements Music 104

Chapter Five: Forming Music Scales 110

Chapter Six: Building Intervals 119

Chapter Seven: Key Signatures 126

Chapter Eight: Building Chords 133

Final Words... 141

Solutions to Exercise Questions 143

Introduction

Thank you and congratulations on purchasing this book, *"Music Theory: For Beginners"* I have written this book to provide you with the steps that you need to take to understand the fundamentals of music theory from a beginner's standpoint.

One of the most common problems that many people face when it comes to music theory is the inability to get a good book that sticks to the fundamental aspects. Music theory is not exactly a topic that will get your heart pounding, so most people want content that will explain music fundamentals in a clear and concise manner. Most music theory books either bore the reader with long, drawn-out explanations, or they toss in some complex concepts that leave you totally confused.

However, this is where this book is different. This book provides you with the only seven exercises that you need as a beginner to master the fundamental elements of written music. These interactive exercises are all based on seven topics that form the basis of every good music theory course. The exercises are spread throughout the book so that once you finish reading each chapter, you can test yourself. I have taken the time to make the questions as challenging as possible yet simple enough for any beginner to understand. In any case, the answers have been provided at the end of the book.

You will not find yourself struggling with complex theories here. I have written this book with the beginner in mind, so every chapter covers a single aspect of music theory. This is to ensure that you move step-by-step, mastering one foundational topic before you move onto the next one. You will learn the common notation system, scales, clefs, key signatures, intervals, chords, and much more.

I have tried to make sure that the topics move sequentially in terms of the level of difficulty. My goal is to take your hand and walk you through every topic and exercise so that you feel comfortable with the content. From my experience with reading and writing music, I know that if you get the first step right, then the next one will automatically fall into place.

By the time you finish reading this book, you will be much more confident in reading and even writing your own music. Yes, it's true! The exercises you will go through in this book will test you and help you grow your musical abilities. I can promise you that with this book, you will finally get to learn all you ever wanted to know about music theory in a fun and interactive way. This is a personal guarantee!

Are you ready? Let's go!

Chapter One: Understanding Music Theory

In this chapter, you will learn about what music theory is all about and why it is important for beginners to have a firm theoretical foundation. You will also go through a brief and painless history of written music. Finally, you will get to discover the seven exercises that are fundamental to the learning of music.

What is Music Theory?

The simplest way to define music theory is this: It is the language that enables you to read, understand, and play any kind of music that has been composed. Music theory is made up of rules and concepts that are designed to govern the way music is written and performed.

Another way to look at it is that music is a language that consists of many various parts. Each part is then divided into smaller sections. If you want to learn how to speak the whole language, you must start by learning the smaller sections first and how to combine them to form the larger parts. Then you must learn how to put together those large parts to communicate whatever message you have through that language.

We learn music theory so that we know how to put the elements together to compose music. That is music theory in a nutshell.

As a beginner, it is easy to fall into the trap of feeling overwhelmed when you hear the words "music theory," but there is really nothing to worry about. The critical thing to keep in mind when learning about music theory is that the music preceded the theory. The art of making musical sounds dates back thousands of years, and at that time, our ancestors didn't have any kind of theory to rely on. They just pounded on their drums and played it by ear. If you are already playing an instrument, then you most likely have a rough idea about music theory. The only issue is that you haven't learned the terms and technicalities yet.

Like I said before, music theory is a language that allows musicians to read and perform compositions the way the composer intended. However, it is important to also note that there are some musicians who are not able to read or write music, yet they can still make awesome melodies and sounds. There are some people who can hear and speak English but cannot read or write it. Therefore, some people view learning music theory as boring and unnecessary.

On the other hand, I believe that a student can progress much further in learning a new language by training himself/herself to read and write it. It is the same with music theory. If you want to master new techniques, gain more confidence, and perform new styles, you need to learn music theory.

Now let's go back a bit into history to unearth the beginnings of music theory.

Musical Beginnings

According to historians, complex musical instruments were already being used as far back as 7000 B.C. Archaeologists have found bone flutes that can still be used to create short performances for modern listeners to hear.

There are pictographs from 3500 B.C. that depict the ancient Egyptians playing clarinets, harps, and lyres. By the year 1500 B.C., the people in Northern Syria had modified the Egyptian harp and created the first ever two-stringed guitar. The instrument even had tuning pegs and a hollow soundboard for amplifying sounds.

So why am I telling you all this?

If you look at the history of ancient music, you will realize that distinct cultures spread out all over the world were able to create music with very similar tonal qualities. How was this possible? It is believed that certain patterns of musical notes just sound right while others do not. If this is the case, then music theory is simply the search for why and how certain notes sound right or wrong. To put it more plainly, music theory is important because it helps us understand *why* an object sounds a particular way and *how* we can reproduce that exact sound.

Ancient Greece is believed to be the origin of music theory. The Greeks even built schools that taught the science and philosophy of analysing music. It was Pythagoras who went as far as creating the 12-pitch octave scale that resembles the one we currently use today. Pythagoras achieved this using a device known as the Circle of Fifths, which you will learn about later in this book.

A lot of the musical theory you are about to learn is based on the works of the ancient Greeks. But unlike the Greek language, this book is much simpler to read and understand.

The Significance of Theory in Your Music

It is easy to think that making great music is as simple as sitting down, playing whatever note you want, going in any direction you see fit, and even stopping at any stage of the performance. That is often the view of most aspiring musicians who would love to play an instrument.

However, such kind of performances, if they do exist, would cause confusion and sound annoying to the listeners. Only those musicians who have thoroughly mastered how to stack notes and chords adjacent to each other can manage to perform a spontaneous jam that listeners would love. In other words, since music is a language that communicates a message, you must learn how to connect with your listeners at all times.

Learning musical theory can also inspire you a great deal, as you will soon find out after you finish reading this book. It is a tremendously great feeling when you discover that you can put together a chord progression and create an awesome song out of it. How would you feel if you could look at a piece of classical music and know that you can play it for the first time?

What about being confident enough to call up your friends and ask them to come over and jam with you? You wouldn't be able to do that without learning music theory since you need a way to communicate with other musicians. You use music theory to talk to one another as you play your various instruments.

The truth is that music theory will broaden your horizons as a musician. If you see yourself as a potential rock guitarist, you will be able to know which notes to play in which key. If it's classical music you are interested in, you will know how to sight-read and maintain a consistent beat. Music is fun but it also requires a prominent level of discipline. At the end of it all, it is worth it!

The Seven Fundamental Exercises

There are a lot of elements that you will have to learn to become an accomplished musician. Of course, we all wish that we could somehow sit down with an instrument and start playing beautiful music without going through the hassle of any formal training. But the reality is that you need structured exercises that will prepare you for your future as a music maestro.

In the next few chapters, we are going to cover music theory fundamentals that will help you get started. There are seven elements that you will have to master to learn these elements effectively. They are:

1. Learning the staff and music alphabet

2. Common notation

3. Basic elements of music (rhythm, melody, harmony, etc)

4. Mastering the scales

5. Building intervals

6. Understanding key signatures

7. Forming chords

Every single one of these elements is critical to your progress as a beginner. They will teach you the individual elements of music and how they are put together to create a solid foundation for reading, playing, and studying music.

Chapter Summary

Here is a summary of the key points of this chapter:

- Music theory is the rules and concepts that enable us to read, understand, and play any kind of musical composition.
- It is possible to play music without learning music theory, but if you want to go further in learning new techniques and performing new styles, you must learn music theory.
- Though complex musical instruments date back as far as 7000 B.C., the ancient Greeks are the ones credited with establishing schools for analysing the elements of music.
- Learning musical theory will enable you to communicate more effectively with listeners and fellow musicians, while also inspiring confidence in your own musical abilities.
- There are seven key exercises that will help you learn the fundamentals of music theory.

In the next chapter, you will learn about the staff and how we use the music alphabet to write music. It isn't a difficult topic, but since the rest of the book will be based on what you learn in the next chapter, you need to make sure that you go through it thoroughly.

Chapter Two: Learning the Staff

In this chapter, you will learn about the staff. It is important to start by learning the main way that we write music. You will learn what the staff looks like, the several types of clefs, and how to arrange notes when writing your music. There will also an exercise at the end of the chapter to test what you have learned.

Human beings started making music way before writing was invented. Even to this day, some musicians choose to play "by ear," which means they don't rely on written music. However, it is important to write music so that it can be shared and studied. This means that we must have system to represent music, hence the need for a music alphabet.

What is the Music Alphabet?

The musical alphabet is an arrangement of letters that enables us to write the sounds that we want to play. Every time you sit down to play music with others, the first thing you do is talk about what you plan on playing. By talking I don't mean just telling each other stories or describing your music verbally. The language of communication should be specific to music, and that is where the music alphabet comes in. The alphabet is the means of representing your music.

Before we go into the musical notes themselves, let's start by learning about the most widespread way of writing music. This is the staff.

The Staff

Now that you have learned about the music alphabet, it's time to tackle a very important component of music. All instruments that play specific pitches are written on the staff, which is comprised of five horizontal parallel lines. Music notes are usually placed either on the lines or in the spaces between the lines. The music on a staff is read from left to right.

In the image below, you will notice some short lines that are above or below the staff. These are known as *ledger lines*. These are used to show a note that is too low or too high to be placed on the staff.

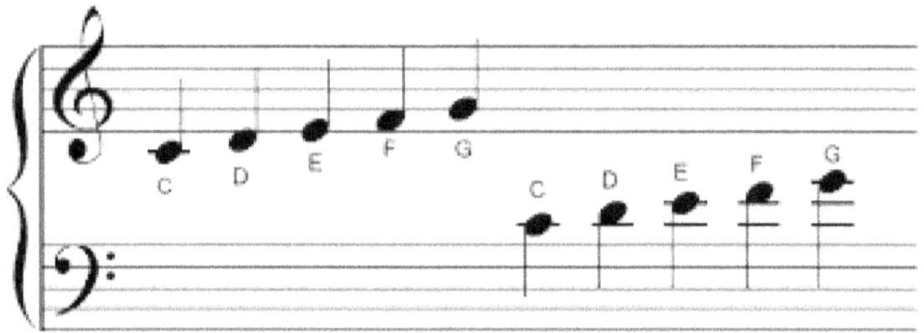

Figure 2.1

To make reading music much easier, vertical lines are used to split the staff into sections. These lines are known as **bar lines**. Each section that is formed on the staff is then called a **measure** or **bar**. At the end of every staff, there are two lines that mark the end of a section of music or song. These are known as **double bar lines**. A heavy double bar line indicates that you have reached the end of the song. A light double bar line means the end of a section of music.

Figure 2.2

You may be wondering what some of the symbols and shapes are on the staff above. These will be discussed later in this chapter.

Clefs

In figure 2.2, you notice a symbol that is placed at the beginning of the staff. This is the *Clef symbol*. It tells you the type of note that is found on every line and space of the staff. There are two kinds of clefs; the treble clef (or G clef) and the bass clef (or F clef).

The reason why it's called a G clef is that its body curls around the line that represents the G note. For the F clef, the symbol curls around the line representing the F note. The notes in the staff are always arranged in ascending order from top to bottom, but they are positioned differently depending on the type of clef being used. The reason why we use different clefs is to cover as many notes within the human voice range as possible, as well as most of the instruments used. People and instruments with high voice ranges use the treble clef while those with lower ranges use bass clef.

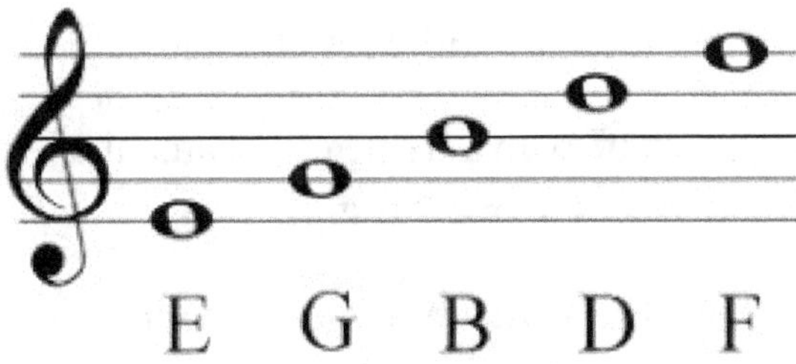

Figure 2.3

Figure 2.4

Exercise 1

1. Draw the staff on a piece of paper and practice writing the two clef symbols on the staff. Draw as many as you can until you learn it perfectly.

2. Draw the staff with treble and name all the spaces on the staff.

3. Draw the staff with bass clef and name the lines in it.

4. On a staff with a treble clef, name the ledger lines and spaces above the staff.

5. On a staff with a bass clef, name the lines and spaces below the staff.

Chapter Summary

Here are some key points you need to remember:

- The musical alphabet is an arrangement of letters that enable us to write the sounds that we want to play.
- The notes on the staff are placed either on the lines or in the spaces between the lines.
- Notes on the staff are arranged in ascending order.
- Ledger lines are used when showing notes that are too high or too low to appear on the staff.
- A bar line splits the staff into sections called measures or bars.
- A heavy double bar line indicates the end of a song.
- A light double bar line indicates the end of a section of music.
- There are two types of clef symbols – the treble clef and the bass clef.

In the next chapter, you will learn about music notation. These are considered the building blocks of music and are necessary when writing your music.

Chapter Three: Understanding Common Notation

In this chapter, you will learn the A-B-C's of the musical language. We will talk about the building blocks that form the foundation of musical theory. These include notes, pitch, octave, beats, and time signature. There will also an exercise at the end of the chapter to test what you have learned.

Common notation simply refers to the standard system that we use to represent music notes. It is more widely used than other types of music notation that have been invented, for example, tablature. You have already learned about one part of common notation in the previous chapter. Now let's talk about notes and pitches.

Notes

Every piece of music you will encounter consists of notes. They are the building blocks of music. A note is simply a letter of the musical alphabet that represents the *pitch* made by a musical instrument.

The pitch of a note refers to how low or high it sounds. Pitch is dependent on the frequency and wavelength of the sound wave of a note. If the frequency of the sound wave is high, and the wavelength is short, the pitch will be high. Since very few musicians are keen on such kind of physics terminologies, they use letters to represent different pitches.

There are seven letters that form the music alphabet. These are:

A B C D E F G A

or:

C D E F G A B C

These seven letters are used to name the white keys on a keyboard. As you can see above, you start with the letter A and proceed to the letter G. After G, instead of going to H, we go back and start counting from A. In music, each set of seven letters (A – G or C - B) is referred to as an *octave*. The moment you reach the eighth note, you begin the next octave.

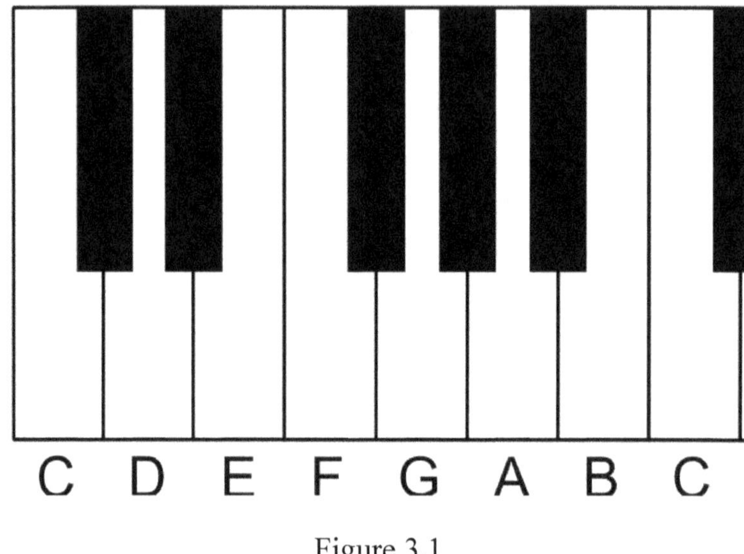

Figure 3.1

But there's one thing that you need to be keenly aware of here. As you move toward the right side, or *up the alphabet*, you realize that you will meet a note with the same letter name as another one before. However, this next note will be at a higher octave than the previous one.

In figure 3.1 above, the second C note has a pitch that is at a higher octave than the first. If you were to move up the alphabet, the third C note would be a higher pitch than the second one, and so on. You can also move in the opposite direction, and this is referred to as going *down the alphabet*.

Sharps and Flats

Though there are only seven letters in the music alphabet, there are more than seven notes. The seven letters from A to G represent *natural* notes. Natural simply means it is a regular note. However, there are five other notes that are usually placed in-between these natural notes. This brings the total number of notes in the music alphabet to 12. These five other notes are represented as *sharp notes* (♯) and *flat notes* (♭).

A sharp note is a note that is higher in pitch than its natural letter. For example, G♯ (pronounced G sharp) is higher than G. On the other hand, a flat note is a note lower than its natural letter, so A♭ (pronounced A flat) is lower in pitch than A. These sharp and flat notes are used to represent the black keys on a keyboard.

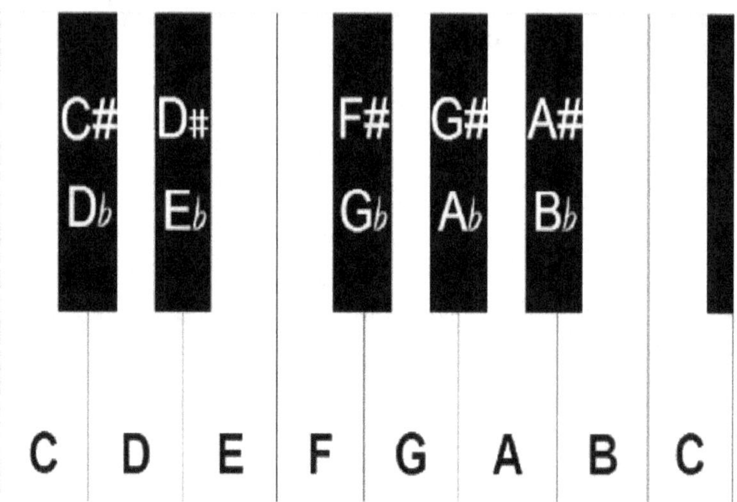

Figure 3.2

From the image above, you can see that in some instances, the sharps and flats occupy the same key. This means that they refer to the same note but are given different names depending on where they are used. This is what is known as ***enharmonics***. In other words, F♯ is the same note as G♭, and C♯ is the same note as D♭, and so on.

If you are keen, you may have noticed that there are some notes that do not have any sharps or flats between them. This happens between the E-F notes and B-C notes. This shouldn't be taken to mean that there is no E♯ or C♭. We simply refer to them as F or B. So, when you raise an E by one note you get an F. Also, when you lower a C note you get a B.

The sharp symbol usually indicates that the particular note is one half-step higher than its natural equivalent. For example, G♯ is one half-step higher than G. In the same way, the flat symbol indicates that the note is one half-step lower than its natural equivalent. So, A♭ is one half-step lower than A.

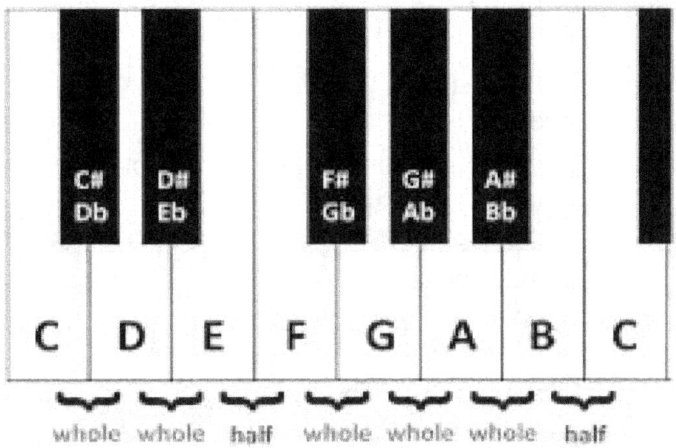

Figure 3.3

In other words, the distance between the G note and the A note is *one whole step*. When you see two adjacent notes having a sharp or a flat note between them, then that means that they are a whole step apart. Therefore, from figure 3.3, it is clear to see that most of the notes on the keyboard are one whole step apart except the E-F notes and B-C notes. These are only one half-step apart.

Parts of a Note

In common notation, sounds are written in form of notes. The two most critical pieces of information that written music should convey to a musician are the pitch to be played and its duration. A note that is placed high on the staff should be played at a higher sound.

To determine the pitch of a note, look at the clef, key signature, and the line or space the note is placed. To determine the duration of a note (how long it lasts), you look at the shape of the note, its tempo, and time signature.

There are three specific parts of a note. There is the head, the stem, and the flag.

- **The Head** (3) – This is the rounded section of a note. The head can be shaded or hollow. Every note must have a head.

- **The Stem** (2) – This is the vertical straight line that is linked to the head. Quavers, crotchets and minims all contain stems. Stems can point either up or down depending on the position of the note on the staff. Notes on or above the centre line have stems pointing down. Notes below the centre line have stems pointing up.

- **The Flag** (1) – This is the line that sticks out from the top or bottom of the stem. Only quavers and shorter notes carry flags.

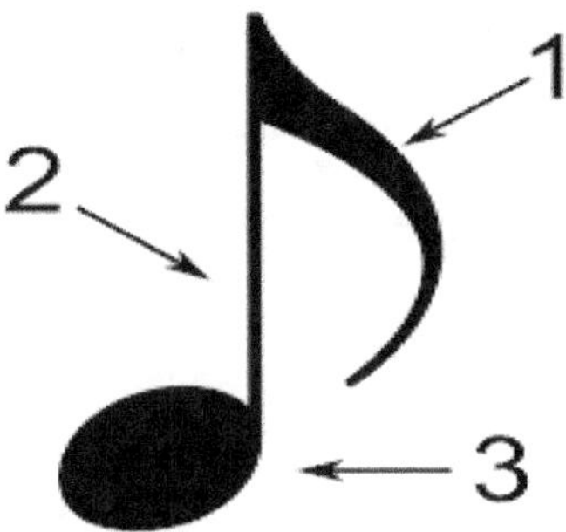

Figure 3.4

The pitch of a note is determined by the position of the head of the note, not the entire body. The head, the stem and the flag are all factors that must be considered when deciding how much time a note is given.

Note Duration and Values

Note duration is defined as the amount of time that a note is played. Each note usually has its own value, and these include the semibreve, minim, crotchet, quaver, and semiquaver. They are shown in this exact order in the image below.

Figure 3.5

The Whole (Semibreve) Note

This note is represented by a hollow oval and has no stem. It is the longest note in modern music and lasts for a full four beats.

This means that for four entire beats, all you must do is play and hold that one note.

The Half (Minim) Note

This is half the value of a semibreve and is held for half as long as the whole note. Two minims occupy the same length of time as a semibreve. It is represented by a hollow oval with a stem.

The Quarter (Crotchet) Note

This is a quarter of a semibreve. Four crotchets occupy the same length of time as a semibreve, which means a crotchet is one beat long. It is represented by a shaded oval with a stem.

The Eighth (Quaver) Note

This is half the length of time as a crotchet. It is represented by a shaded oval with a stem and a flag. The flag cuts the value of a note by half.

The Sixteenth (Semiquaver) Note

Two semiquavers occupy the same length of time as one quaver. It is represented by a shaded oval with a stem and two flags.

If two notes that have flags are next to each other, they are sometimes connected using a *beam*. This makes it possible to group flagged notes so that the music is easier and faster to read. The same principle also applies to semiquavers. A note must have the same number of beams as it does flags.

Figure 3.6: Semiquaver with beam

Dotted Notes

By now you know that a minim is half the length of a semibreve; a crotchet is half of a minim, and so on. But what do you do if you want a note length that is not half of another note? That's where the dotted note comes in. A dotted note is 1 ½ times the length of the same note. So, you end up with the original note length and half of that note length. For example, a dotted minim would have a duration that is as long as a minim plus a crotchet; or three crotchets.

If a note has two dots, it simply means that each dot adds half the length of the previous note. This is shown in figure 3.7 below.

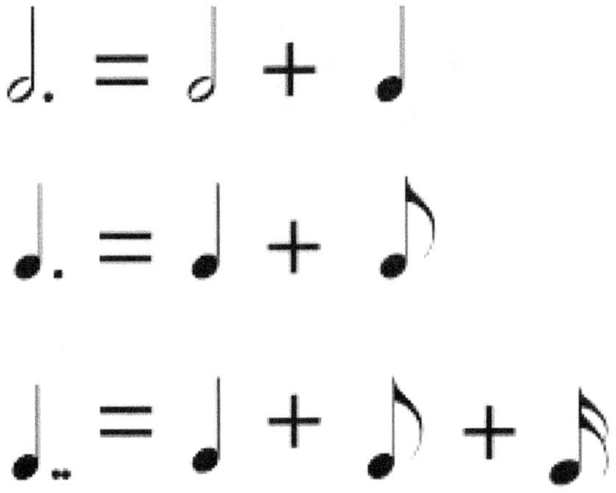

Figure 3.7

Time Signatures

These are usually indicated at the front end of the staff and are placed after the clef symbol and key signature. The time signature doesn't appear on every staff. It is used only when there is a change in the meter. *Meter* refers to the basic rhythm of the music. Time signature represents the meter and tells you how you should write it.

A fraction represents time signatures. The number at the top indicates the number of beats per measure while the number at the bottom indicates the type of note that will be used to carry the beat. The next section explains this more clearly.

Figure 3.7

Beats

There are many ways to organize music, and one of them is by splitting the time into small periods known as ***beats***. Most of the actions that go with a piece of music occur at the start of the beat. For example, when you tap your foot or clap your hands, you are making those sounds or movements at the start of the beat. This is usually referred to as being "on the downbeat" since it corresponds to the moment when the conductor's baton reaches the bottom of its path.

The downbeat is the most substantial section of a beat, though some are stronger than the rest. Beats form a pattern such as strong-weak-weak-strong-weak-weak. Therefore, beats are further grouped into measures or bars. For example, a beat such as strong-weak-weak-strong-weak-weak would be written as 1-2-3-1-2-3, which means that each measure must contain three beats.

We already talked about how time signature indicates the number of beats per measure and the kind of note that carries a beat. For example, figure 3.7 has a time signature that requires three quarter (crotchet) notes in all the measures on that particular staff. In other words, every measure will have three crotchets. We usually say that such a piece is in "three four" time.

Don't forget what we learned earlier. A crotchet (quarter) note is one beat long. In other words, every measure on the staff should have the equivalent of three beats. These can still be represented as one minim and a crotchet, or six quavers per measure.

Exercise 2

1. Complete the following series of natural notes: A B
   _ _ E F _ _

2. Provide an alternative name for the following:

   a. A♯

   b. D♭

   c. G♭

   d. E♭

Fill in the blanks:

3. 1 semibreve = _____________ quavers

4. 1 minim = _____________ quarters

5. 1 minim = 1 quarter + _____________ eighths

6. Draw two staves with a treble clef symbol and time signatures showing *two four-time, three eight time,* and *six four time.* Fill in each measure with a different combination of note lengths. Use at least one dotted note in each staff.

Chapter Summary

Here are some of the key points you need to remember:

- A note is a letter that represents the pitch made by a musical instrument.
- An octave is a set of notes from one letter to the next pitch by the same letter name.
- The symbol ♯ represents sharp notes.
- Flat notes are represented by the symbol ♭.
- Enharmonics are two notes that have equal pitches but are known by different names.
- There are five note values - semibreve, minim, quarter, quaver, and semiquaver. Each note lasts half the beat of the previous one.
- Music is divided into short time periods called beats.
- The time signature is shown using a fraction. The number at the top indicates the number of beats per measure. The number at the bottom indicates the type of note that will be used to carry the beat.

In the next chapter, you will learn about the building blocks of music. These are the basic elements of every musical piece, and they include aspects like rhythm, harmony, melody, timbre, and dynamics.

Chapter Four: The Basic Elements Music

In this chapter, you will learn about the essential elements that make music what it really is. These are aspects that even non-musicians can understand. As long as you have an appreciation for good music, you should be able to pick out these musical building blocks.

We are going to cover a number of these basic elements here. It is also important to note that musical theory experts hold differing opinions as to the total number of the elements of music. Some claim that there are as few as four while others say that there are as many as 10. Here we shall be covering rhythm, harmony, melody, timbre, texture, and dynamics.

Creating Rhythm

The primary reason why we study music theory is to be able to describe different musical pieces regarding how similar or different they are about the above six elements. Rhythm is considered one of the most basic components of any kind of music. Some types of music don't have harmony or melody, but every piece of music must have rhythm.

So, what exactly is rhythm?

Rhythm can be defined as the pattern of sounds repeated throughout the music. We can also say that rhythm is the arrangement of note lengths in music. Music and time go hand in hand, which means that rhythm has to be heard over a period of time. Rhythm is usually shaped by the meter and incorporates other elements such as *tempo* and *beat*.

Tempo is the speed at which you play a particular piece of music. When creating a composition, you indicate the tempo using an Italian word. For example, if you look at the starting point of a score, you may see words like *Largo* (slow pace), *Moderato* (moderate pace), or *Presto* (very fast pace). Here are some common tempo markings and their translations:

- Adagio – slow

- Vivo – lively and brisk

- Lento – slow

- Molto – a lot

- Mosso – motion or movement

- Piu – more

- Allegro – fast

- (un) poco – a little

- Meno – less

Harmony

Harmony is the result of having more than one pitch being heard at the same time. When you hear two or more notes being played at one time, you are listening to harmony. Harmony provides support for the melody and gives it texture. Harmony is usually described as being diminished, augmented, major, and minor.

Melody

Melody can be described as the general tune that is created when you play a succession of notes. It is influenced by your rhythm and pitch. A musical piece can have just one melody running through it, or it may have several melodies stacked in a verse-chorus form.

Timbre

Timbre is the quality of a sound that differentiates one musical instrument or voice from another. It is also called *tone color*. Timbre has nothing to do with the volume, length, or pitch of a sound.

For example, if you play a specific note on a clarinet and then on an oboe for five seconds at a specific volume, a listener can easily know that the notes are different. This is because the timbre of a clarinet is different from that of an oboe.

Texture

This refers to the type and number of layers that are used in a musical composition. Texture can be a single melodic line (monophonic), several melodic lines (polyphonic), or the main melody together with chords (homophonic).

Dynamics

This is the intensity that a musical piece is performed. In written music, dynamics are represented by symbols or abbreviations that indicate the volume that a note should be sung or played. Just like tempo, dynamics are derived from Italian words. For example, *fortissimo* indicates an extremely loud passage while *pianissimo* indicates an extremely soft section of music.

Here are some typical dynamic markings:

- mf mezzo forte   = medium loud

- f   forte   = loud

- ff fortissimo   = very loud

- fff fortississimo = very, very loud

- p   piano   = soft

- pp pianissimo   = very soft

- mp mezzo piano = medium soft

Exercise 3

1. Test yourself and see whether you can interpret what these Italian tempo markings mean:

   - Poco pin mosso

   - Piu vivo

   - Un poco allegro

   - Molto adagio

2. Write these dynamics in order from the quietest to the loudest: f, p, mf, ff, pp, and mp

Chapter Summary

Here are some of the key points you need to remember:

- Rhythm is the pattern of sounds repeated throughout the music.
- Rhythm depends on the tempo and beat of the music
- Tempo refers to the pace of the music and is usually indicated by Italian words.
- Harmony is created when more than one pitch is played at the same time.
- Melody is the general tune created when a succession of notes is played. A musical piece can have one or more melodies.
- Timbre is what tells us the difference between sounds made by different instruments.
- Texture is the number and type of layers in a musical composition. It can be monophonic, polyphonic, or homophonic.
- Dynamics is the intensity that music is played, and its markings are derived from Italian words.

In the next chapter, you will learn more about the different types of music scales. These are considered to be subsets of the notes you learned in Chapter 3.

Chapter Five: Forming Music Scales

In this chapter, you will learn how to create the different types of music scales. You will start with the simplest one, which is the major scale, and then proceed onto the more complex minor scale.

Music scales can be described as a set of notes arranged in sequential order, chosen to be used for a particular song. Why do we choose those notes? Simply because they sound great together! Though different cultures have adopted a variety of scales, the most common one is the major scale.

In order to create a scale, you need to go through the music alphabet (remember the seven letters from A to G?) and pick out notes that go well together. The notes chosen must achieve a particular sound. In most cases, you can do this by combining whole steps and half steps.

Tonal Centre

Every scale begins with the note that it is named after. That particular note is referred to as the **_tonal centre_** of that scale, and it is where the music in that scale feels "at rest."

For example, in most cases, music in the C major scale always ends on a C major chord. The music will begin on the C note, return to the C note repeatedly, and the melody will be based on the C note so much that listeners be able to identify where the tonal centre of that piece of music is.

Major Scales

If you have ever heard a song that sounds cheerful, uplifting, and fun, then it was probably written in a major key. Music that is written using a particular key only uses some of the many notes available. This sequence of notes then forms what we call a scale. Major keys are used to build major chords to then form a major scale.

It is important to know that different songs can use different scales, and different parts of a song can also make use of different scales. Scales are normally written in a sequential order from one note to the next note of the same letter. For example, we can have a scale that ranges from note C to the next note C, as shown below.

C D E F G A B C

As we already learned, each set of seven letters of the music alphabet forms an octave. Therefore, we can say that the above scale is a one-octave scale. To create a two-octave scale, you simply continue the same sequence until you land on the next note with the same letter name.

C D E F G A B C D E F G A B C

The range of notes from C to C is what forms the scale for C major. None of the notes in this particular scale has a sharp or a flat. On the other hand, the D major scale has two sharps. These are F sharp and C sharp.

D E F♯ G A B C♯ D

So, the question you are probably asking is: How are we supposed to know which notes should be sharpened and which ones should be flattened? The first method involves the use of a chart. However, this can be a cumbersome way since you have to keep referring all the time. You may even be forced to cram all that information into your head. The better alternative is to learn how to use whole and half steps.

Whole Steps and Half Steps

We talked about how the pitch of a sound represents how high or low the sound is. In music, we usually say that one note is either much higher or lower than another. This distance between two pitches is known as a half step. If you look at figure 5.1 below, you will be able to understand this better. This method of counting up whole and half steps can be used to form music scales from scratch.

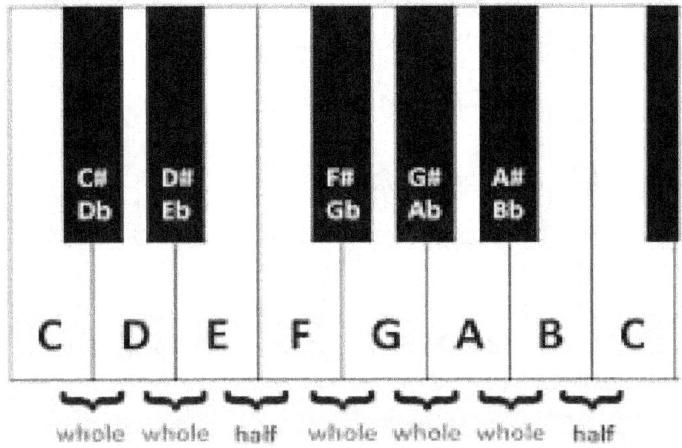

Figure 5.1

For example, we know that the distance from A to A♯ is a half step. The distance between B and B♭ is a half step. In other words, two consecutive half steps form a whole step. The format of any major scale usually follows this kind of sequence:

whole whole half whole whole whole half

This can also be written as:

w w h w w w h

This sequence means that there is a whole step between the first and second note, the second and third note, the fourth and fifth note, the fifth and sixth note, and the sixth and seventh note. There is a half step between the third and fourth note and the seventh and eighth note.

Please memorize this pattern because every major scale you encounter from here onwards will use this same sequence.

So, if we want to form the C major scale, we can write it as:

C w D w E h F w G w A w B h C

Figure 5.2

However, if we want to form the D major scale, we can write it as:

D w E w F♯ h G w A w B w C♯ h D

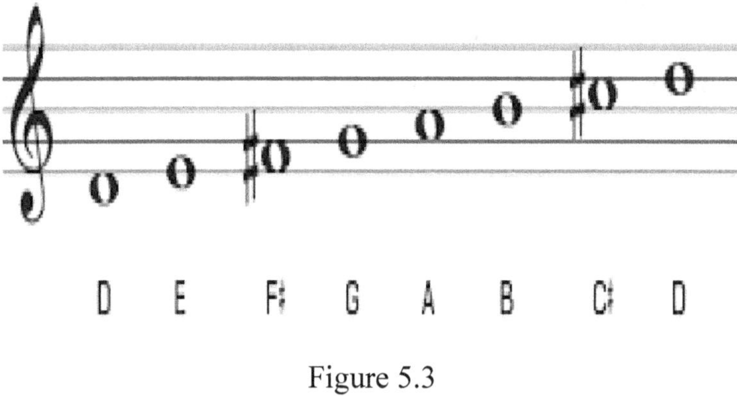

Figure 5.3

Minor Scales

Most people think of minor scales as confusing. This is because many music students usually start learning about the major scale first and end up focusing on it more than the minor scale. This situation isn't helped by the fact that there are a number of different types of minor scales that are often confused with one another. However, we will only focus on the most common minor scale in this book.

It is important to note that a piece of music in a particular major scale will sound the same as music in another major scale. For example, music that is in C major will sound somewhat similar to music in D major.

However, music in D major will sound very different from that in D minor because the notes in a minor scale are arranged in a very different pattern. Music written using a minor key has a sad, ominous, or mysterious sound than that written using a major key.

Natural Minor Scale

A natural minor scale is a scale where every note is played in a minor key signature. A natural minor scale is formed by starting at the tonal centre and moving upward using the following step pattern:

Whole half whole whole half whole whole

w h w w h w w

For example, music written in D minor scale will look like this:

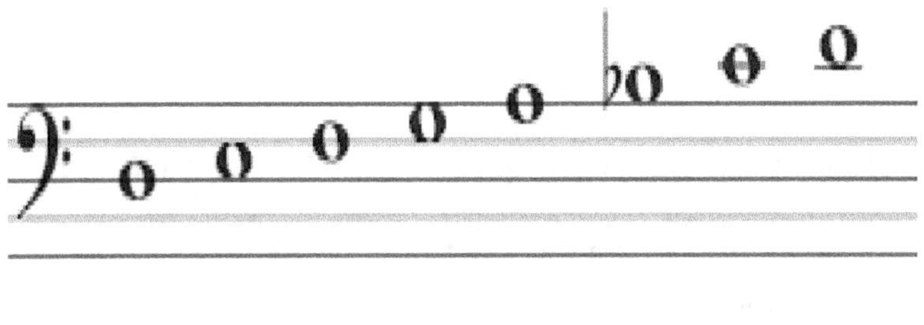

Figure 5.4

Exercise 4

1. Draw a staff with a treble clef. Write down the notes of the A major scale.

2. Draw a staff with a bass clef. Write down the notes of the G flat major scale.

3. Draw a staff with a treble clef. Write down the notes of the F minor scale.

4. Draw a staff with a treble clef. Write down the notes of the A flat minor scale.

Chapter Summary

Here are the key points to remember from this chapter:

- A music scale is a set of notes that sound good together, arranged in sequential order, within a particular piece of music.
- The tonal centre is the first note in a scale and is used to name that particular scale.
- To remember the sequence of notes in a major scale, follow the pattern *w w h w w w h*.
- A natural minor scale is written in a minor key and follows the pattern *w h w w h w w*.

In the next chapter, you will learn about the different types of intervals and how they are built.

Chapter Six: Building Intervals

In this chapter, you will learn about the different types of intervals and how to name them. Intervals are a very important concept in music. In fact, you cannot learn about scales or chords without making some reference to intervals. As a serious student of music theory, you must take the time to learn intervals and how to identify them.

Defining Intervals

An interval can be defined as the distance or space between two notes or pitches. Intervals are described using whole steps and half steps, which we have already covered in the previous chapters. The uncomplicated way to describe an interval would be to say, "E natural is one-half step below F natural," or "A flat is one step and a half away from F."

However, these are small distances. What about when we need to describe longer intervals in a major or minor scale?

How to Name Intervals

The primary factor you have to consider when naming an interval is the distance between the two notes. You need to look at how the notes are presented and then count the spaces and lines between the notes in the staff. Make sure that you include the spaces or lines that the notes are positioned on.

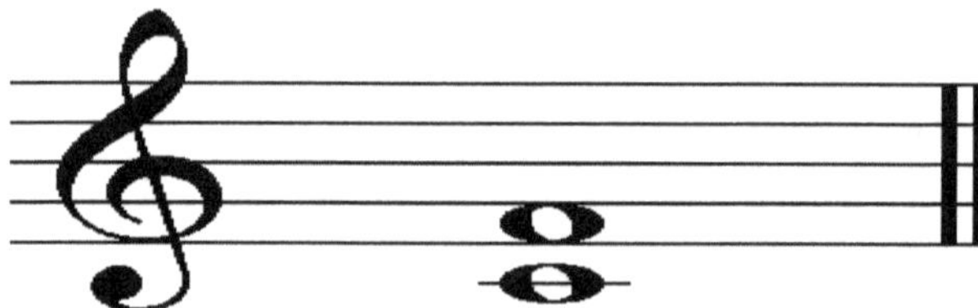

Figure 6.1

Figure 6.2

In figure 6.1 above, the interval between the C and F notes is four. We refer to this *a fourth*. In figure 6.2, the interval count between C and E is a third. At this point, the type of clef, key signature, and accidental (flats and sharps) don't matter.

If the interval between the notes is less or equal to one octave, it is referred to as a **simple interval** *(fig 6.3)*. If the interval is greater than one octave, it is called a **compound interval** *(fig 6.4)*.

Figure 6.3

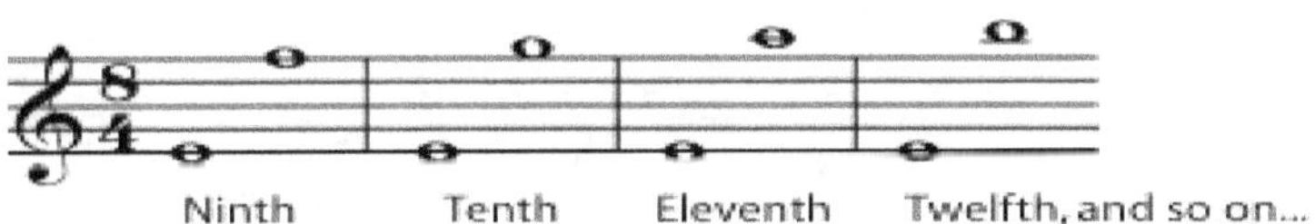

Figure 6.4

Now in the next phase of identifying an interval, we will consider the clef, key signature, and accidentals.

Perfect Intervals

Certain intervals are considered to be perfect intervals. They include primes, fourths, fifths, and octaves. They are called perfect because their sound waves are related very closely to one another. This makes these intervals sound good together.

Another name for a perfect prime is ***unison,*** which represents two notes that produce the same pitch. A perfect fourth has 5 half steps and a perfect fifth has 7 half steps. A perfect octave is where two notes are eight intervals apart, that is, 12 half steps apart. It is important that you understand how these steps are counted. You can go back and refresh your knowledge from the previous chapter on scales.

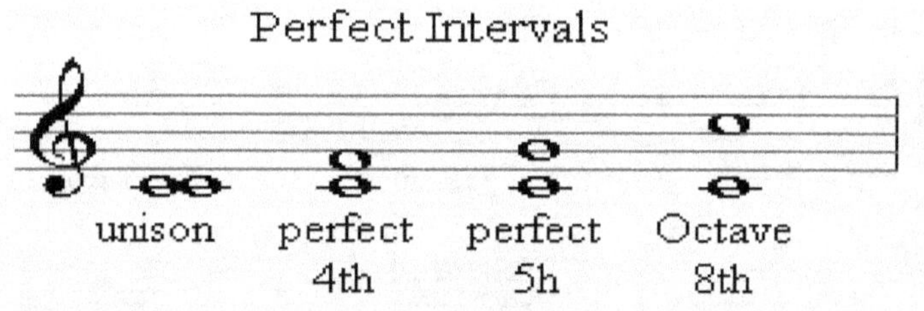

Figure 6.5

Major and Minor Intervals

The rest of the simple intervals form the major and minor intervals. These include seconds, thirds, sixths, and sevenths. A minor interval is one half-step smaller than a major one. They are described as follows:

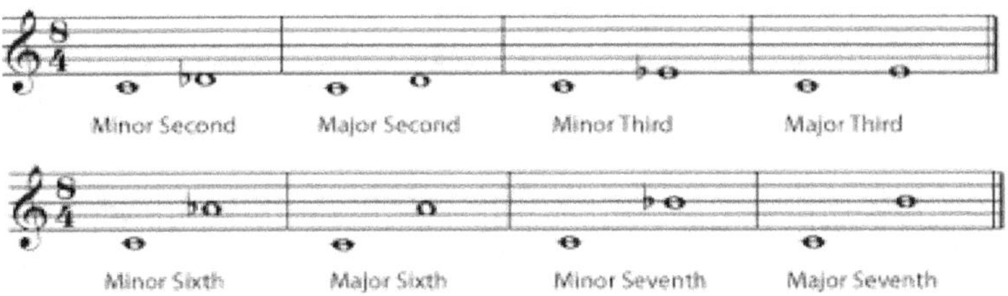

Figure 6.6

- Minor second – 1 half step

- Major second – 2 half steps

- Minor third – 3 half steps

- Major third – 4 half steps

- Minor sixth – 8 half steps

- Major sixth – 9 half steps

- Minor seventh – 10 half steps

- Major seventh – 11 half steps

Exercise 5

1. Give the complete name of the intervals.

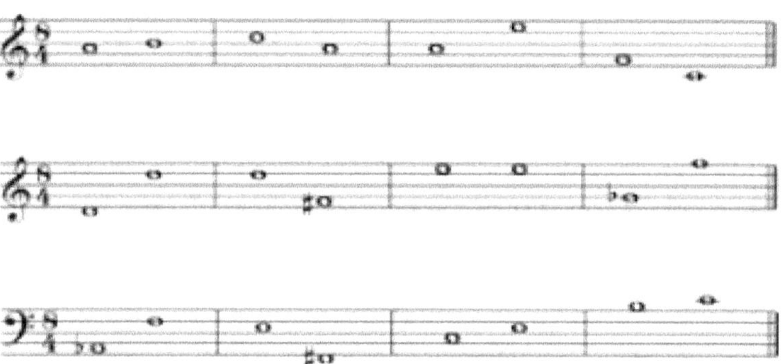

Chapter Summary

Here are the key points that you need to remember:

- Interval is the distance between two pitches.
- In order to name an interval, count the lines and spaces between the two notes. Don't forget to include the line or space the notes are standing on.
- The second phase of naming an interval must consider the half steps. The clef, key signature, and accidentals are important here.
- A simple interval is one octave or smaller, while a compound interval is greater than one octave.
- Intervals are considered perfect if their sound waves are closely related. Perfect intervals include primes, fourths, fifths, and octaves
- A perfect prime is also called unison.
- A minor interval is one half-step smaller than a major interval. These intervals include seconds, thirds, sixths, and sevenths.

In the next chapter, you will learn about key signatures and the circle of fifths.

Chapter Seven: Key Signatures

In this chapter, you will learn about how to use key signatures to make the performance of music much easier. You will also learn about the major and minor key signatures as well as how to read the circle of fifths.

Key signatures are a very important part of music. The key signature is what we use to know the pitches that a song will be performed. Every time that a piece of music is performed, it is played in a particular key or tonality. For example, if a song is to be played using the D key, then the entire song must be based around a D chord or a D note. Even the notes used will be from a D scale. The key signature represents all this information.

So how do we know the key that is being used?

If you look at the beginning of every line of written music, you will notice that there are sharps or flats (also known as accidentals) right after the clef symbol. These accidentals tell us the key to use. It is important to note that a key can either be a sharp or a flat, but it can never be both.

So, what is the significance of using keys? When you are writing a long piece of music in a single key, you will soon find it very tedious to keep repeating the accidentals all over the staff. Look at the image below to see what a simple melody in D major looks like if you don't use a key signature.

Figure 7.1

Now, this is just a short section of a piece of music. If you were writing a full song, the staff would get quite messy, not to mention the fact that you would get tired of writing all those sharps. So, to avoid this, music composers use key signatures only at the beginning of the staff to show the performers which pitches must have accidentals.

Below is the same simple melody in D major. But this time it has a key signature that indicates that the notes C and F should be sharpened.

Figure 7.2

The Circle of Fifths

This is a graphical way of arranging keys to show how closely related they are to each other. The circle of fifths has been part of music theory for centuries, and it provides a great method for summarizing the key signatures to be used for any key that has a maximum of seven sharps or flats.

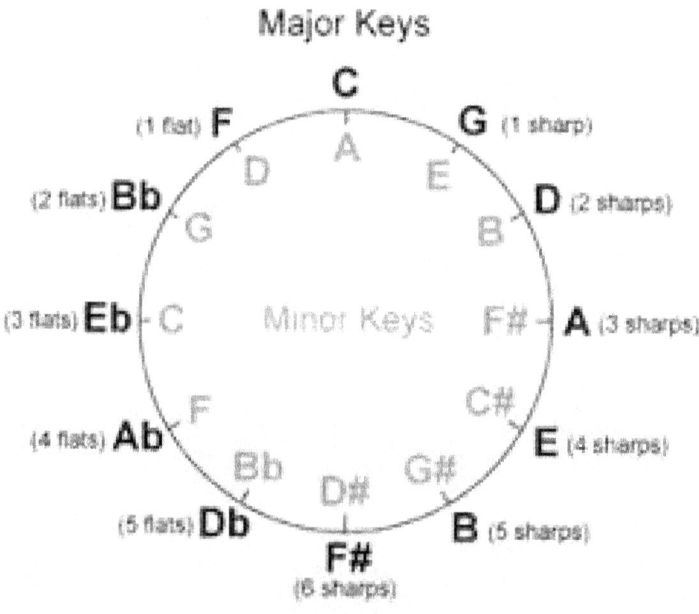

Figure 7.3

So how will you know which notes in the key are supposed to be sharpened or flattened? In order to use the circle of fifths to identify your key signature, you must use a mnemonic device to help you memorize the order of sharps and flats.

The first thing to do is memorize the order of notes on the following circle:

F C G D A E B

Most people use the mnemonic *Father Charles Goes Down And Ends Battle*

If you want to determine the sharp keys, you move clockwise around the circle of fifths. Then you read the mnemonic forward. For example, according to the circle of fifths, there are three sharps in the key A major. But which notes exactly are supposed to be sharp?

Moving clockwise along the circle and following the order of notes, you will identify the notes to be sharpened as F, C, and G.

If you want to determine the flat keys, you must move anticlockwise along the circle, and then read the mnemonic backward. For example, according to the circle of fifths, there are four flats in the key for A-flat major. But which notes should be flattened?

Moving anticlockwise along the circle and backward along the order of notes, you will see that B, E, A, and D are the notes that will have flats.

The reason why we call it a circle of fifths is because as you move from one section (or key) to the next, you are moving down or up by an interval of a perfect fifth. If you move clockwise by a perfect fifth, you will land on a key with one sharp more or one flat less than where you started. If you move anticlockwise a perfect fifth, you land on a key that has one flat more or one sharp less than where you started.

Minor Key Signatures

So far, we have been focusing more on the major keys. However, minor keys also have signatures. Every major key you see on the circle of fifths has a corresponding minor key with the exact same signature. Minor and major keys that have corresponding key signatures are referred to as ***relative keys***. For example, both F major and D minor have one flat. F major is regarded as the relative major of D minor while D minor is regarded as the relative minor of F major.

In other words, just because keys are next to each other on a keyboard (the chromatic scale) does not mean that they are closely related. The main factor that determines the relationship is having similar key signatures. The closer the keys are in the circle of fifths, the closer their relationship in terms of key signature.

This means that the next most closely related keys to F major and D minor are C major (or A minor), and B major (or G minor). Those keys that don't correspond at all with the key signature of F major are on the opposite side of the circle.

Exercise 6

1. Which keys in the circle of fifths are closely related to F sharp major and B flat major?

2. Name the major and minor keys for each key signature.

Chapter Summary

Here are the key points to remember:

- Key signatures tell us the pitches that a song will be performed in.
- To make writing music much easier, the key signature is placed at the beginning of the staff instead of between the notes in the staff.
- The accidentals indicate the key to be used in a piece of music.
- The circle of fifths is a graphical illustration of keys and indicates how closely related they are to each other.
- To determine the key being used, look at the number of sharps or flats in the key signature.
- To identify key signatures, use the mnemonic Father Charles Goes Down And Ends Battle (FCGDAEB).
- To identify the sharp keys, move clockwise around the circle and read the mnemonic forwards.
- To identify the flat keys, move anticlockwise and read the mnemonic backward.
- Major and minor keys that have corresponding key signatures are known as relative keys.

In the next chapter, you will learn about triads, chords, and chord progressions.

Chapter Eight: Building Chords

In this chapter, you will learn chords, which are the building blocks of the tone of a piece of music. Learning how to build chords can be a bit challenging for beginners, but the trick lies in taking it one step at a time. For that reason, we are going to focus on building triads, major chords, and minor chords.

Chords

A chord is simply a group of notes that are played together. Most of the sad songs you hear use what are known as minor chords. The upbeat songs tend to use suspended second chords or major seventh chords. Chords can either be used to make melodies or they can be arranged in specific sequences known as progressions to create a sense of direction and movement in music.

Triads

Chords are a set of three or more pitches that are played together. A chord that is made up of three notes that can be arranged as thirds is known as a ***triad***. The fastest way to know if a chord of three notes is a triad is to arrange the notes in a circle of thirds. If the pitch classes of the three notes sit next to each other, then they form a triad.

There are two ways of identifying a triad, i.e., according to its root and its quality. The ***root of chord,*** which is the note that gives the chord its name, is the lowest note. The second note in the triad is known as the ***third of chord***, while the last note in the triad is called the ***fifth of chord***. After you position the root of chord, you then place the third of chord a third higher than the root. The fifth of chord is then placed a fifth higher than the root, which coincides with a third higher than the third of chord. If you find this confusing, you may need to go to Chapter 6 (figure 6.3) where we learned about intervals.

In the figure below, the chord is written in the root position as a stack of third, which is the easiest way to write down a triad. Don't forget that in most cases, the root is the bottom note, unless you are dealing with an inversion.

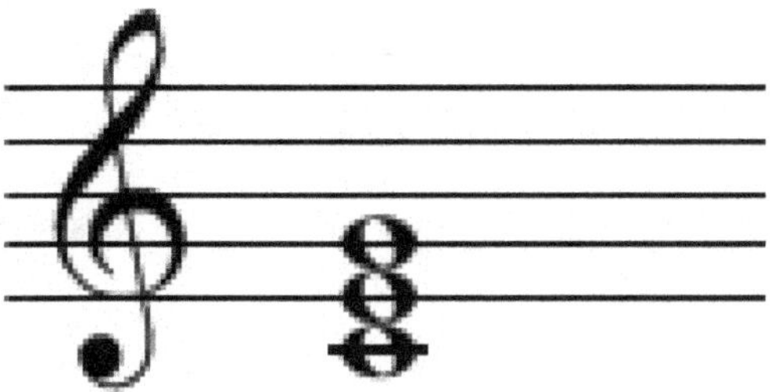

Figure 8.1

First and Second Inversions

First inversion occurs when the third of chord becomes the lowest note. In case the fifth of chord is placed at the bottom, then the chord is said to be in *second inversion*. The second inversion is also known as a *six-four chord* because the intervals are a sixth and a fourth.

The most important factor in a chord is not the distance between the top two notes from the lowest note. The number of notes also isn't an issue. The thing that matters the most is which note is at the bottom.

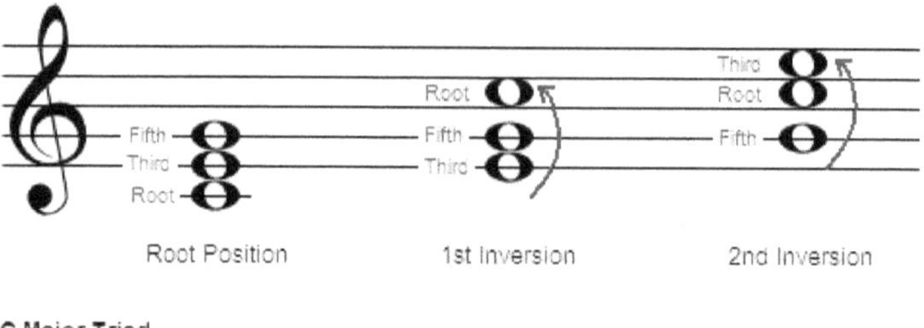

Figure 8.2

Triad Qualities

The first step in determining the quality of a triad is to identify the interval between the root and the other notes in the chord. The four qualities of triads that can be found in major and minor scales include:

- Major triad – M3 and P5 above root

- Minor triad – m3 and p5 above root

- Diminished triad – m3 and d5 above root

- Augmented triad – M3 and A5 above root

The two most common triads are the major and minor chords. In these two types of chords, the root of the chord and fifth of chord are at an interval of a perfect fifth, which are 7 half steps. This interval can be split into a major third, which is 4 half-steps, and a minor third, which forms 3 half-steps.

A ***major chord*** is formed when the major third falls between the root and the third of chord. A ***minor chord*** is formed when the minor third falls between the root and the third of chord.

On the other hand, diminished and augmented chords do not have a perfect fifth, which explains why they produce an anxious feeling in listeners. **Augmented chords** are formed when two major thirds are combined, thus creating an augmented fifth. **Diminished chords** are formed when two minor thirds are combined, thus creating a diminished fifth.

Figure 8.3

Seventh Chords

This is a chord that is formed when you take a triad and combine it with a note that is a seventh above the root. There are many different varieties of seventh chords, and we distinguish them according to the type of seventh and type of triad used. Here are some of the most common types of seventh chords:

- Dominant seventh chord – This is a combination of a major triad and a minor seventh

- Minor seventh chord – This is a combination of a
  minor triad and a minor seventh

- Major seventh chord – This is a combination of a
  major triad and a major seventh

- Diminished seventh chord – This is a combination of
  a diminished triad and a diminished seventh

- Half-diminished seventh chord – This is a
  combination of a diminished triad and a minor
  seventh

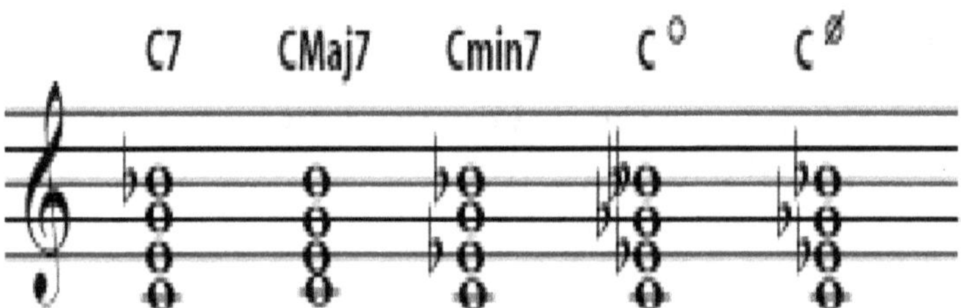

Figure 8.4

Exercise 7

1. Write these seventh chords – G minor seventh; B flat major seventh; F sharp minor seventh; and D diminished seventh.

Chapter Summary

Here are some of the key points that you need to remember:

- A chord is a group of notes that are played together.
- A chord that comprises three notes arranged as thirds is known as a triad.
- Its root and quality can identify a triad.
- In a triad, the lowest note is the root of chord; the second note is the third of chord, and the last note is the fifth of chord.
- First inversion occurs when the third of chord becomes the lowest note.
- Second inversion occurs when the fifth of chord becomes the lowest note.
- When the interval between the root and third of chord is the major third, a major chord is formed.
- When the interval between the root and third of chord is the minor third, a major chord is formed.
- When two major thirds are combined, an augmented chord is formed.

- When two minor thirds are combined, a diminished chord is formed.
- A seventh chord is formed when you add a triad and a note that is a seventh above the root.

Final Words

You have come to the end of the book. Though it was a long journey, I'm sure you now have a much better understanding of music theory than before. If you had never studied the subject previously, you should be ready to move on to the more complex theories of music. If you already had a background in music, then your knowledge of music theory will help you become an even better musician. For those who were seeking a refresher course in some of the elements you had forgotten, consider your mind refreshed.

Music theory is not really as hard as it looks or sounds. The bottom line is that you have to have a solid foundation that will always be there to guide you. The seven elements of music we have covered in this book are the keys to unlocking any musical composition. On top of that, there are seven good exercises in this book that will help you crystallize the knowledge you have gained in each chapter.

The questions provided in every exercise have covered the fundamentals that every music student and musician must know like the back of their hand. If you were keen when reading the book, I'm sure you had an easy time answering them. If you felt like you were struggling a little bit, then don't worry about it. Just go back to the chapter where you feel uncertain and reread it. Some of the concepts usually take time to sink in. Don't forget that the answers to every question are on the last page of the book.

Being able to read and write music is a very rewarding experience, and now you are ready to move onto the next phase of your musical journey. Yes, that was the easy part. Anybody can buy a book, read it, and toss it aside. All it will cost you is some time and money. However, you must now do the hard work necessary to integrate and incorporate this new knowledge into your music. This book has provided you with an opportunity to learn something that can help you going forward. Don't stop here. What is important is that you continue to practice and challenge yourself. Never stop learning and always make an effort to put into practice everything that you have learned in this book.

I am honoured that you took the time to read this book. It was a pleasure for me to walk with you through your musical journey. I hope you enjoyed reading and learning from this beginner's guide to music theory.

Thank you and good luck!

Solutions to Exercise Questions

Solutions to Exercise 1

1. Draw the staff on a piece of paper and practice writing
    the two clef symbols on the staff. Draw as many as you
    can until you learn it perfectly.

2. Draw the staff with a treble clef and name all the spaces
    on the staff.

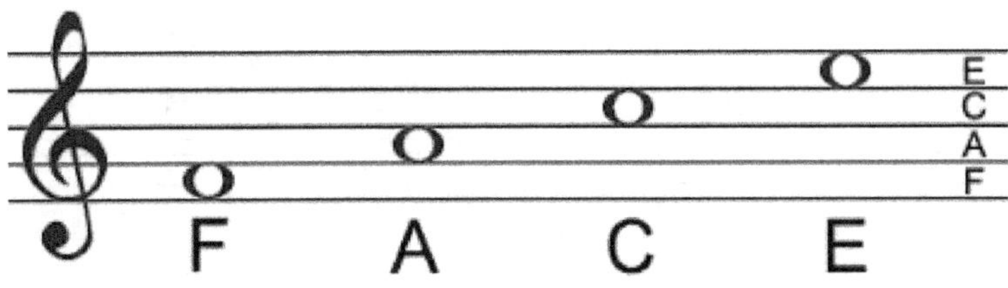

3. Draw the staff with a bass clef and name all the lines on it.

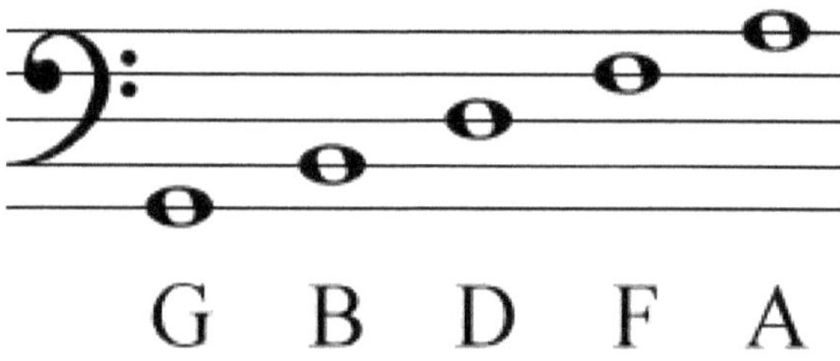

4. On a staff with a treble clef, name the ledger lines and spaces above the staff.

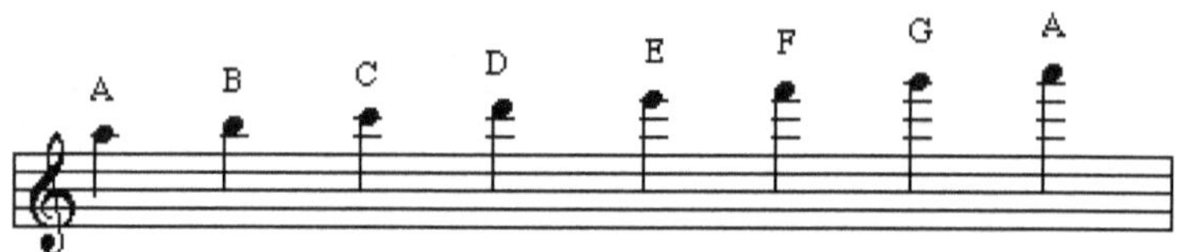

5. On a staff with a bass clef, name the ledger lines and spaces below the staff.

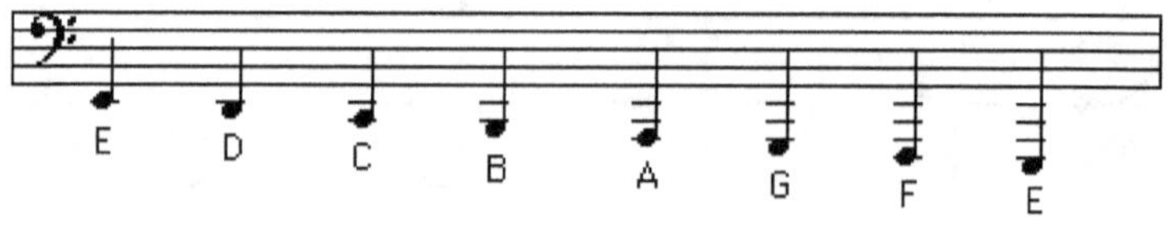

Solutions to Exercise 2

1. Complete the following series of natural notes: A B C D
   E F G A

2. Provide an alternative name for the following:

A♯ - B ♭

D♭ - C♯

G♭ - F♯

E♭ - D♯

3. 1 semibreve = 8 quavers

4. 1 minim = 4 quarters

5. 1 minim = 1 quarter + 2 eighths

6. Three staves with a treble clef symbol and time
   signatures showing *two four time, three eight time,* and
   six four time. Fill in each measure with a different
   combination of note lengths. Use at least one dotted note
   per staff.

Solutions to Exercise 3

1. Italian tempo markings:

   - Poco piu mosso – a little more movement/motion

   - Piu vivo – more lively

   - Un poco allegro – a little fast

   - Molto adagio – very slow

2. In order from quietest to loudest: pp, mp, p, f, mf, ff

Solutions to Exercise 4

1. The staff with a treble clef and notes of the A major scale.

2. The staff with a bass clef and notes of the G flat major scale.

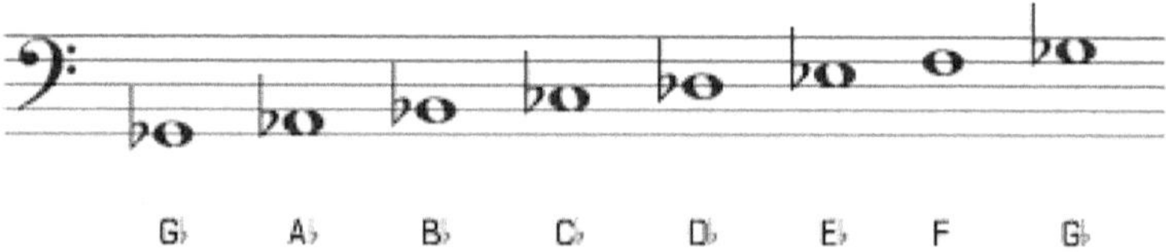

3. The staff with a treble clef and notes of the F minor scale.

F minor scale

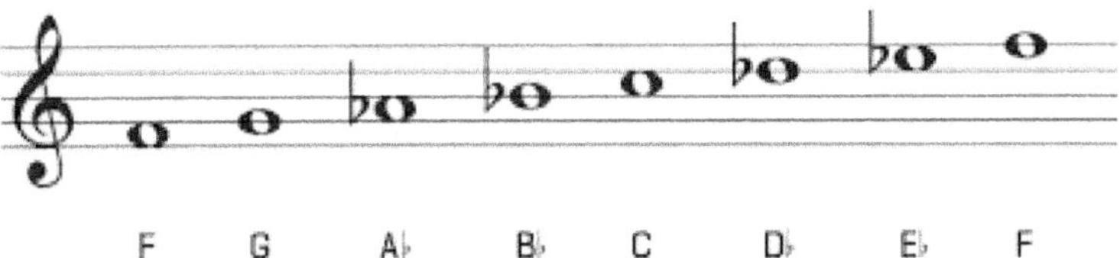

4. The staff with a treble clef and notes of the A flat minor scale.

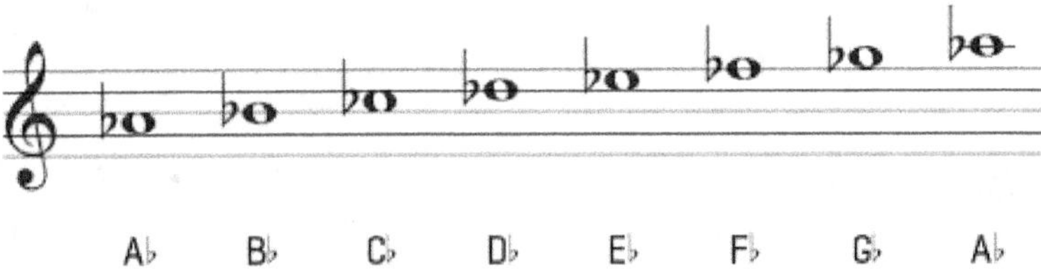

Solutions to Exercise 5

Names of intervals:

Top Staff:

Major Second - Minor Third - Perfect Fifth - Perfect Fourth

Centre Staff:

Perfect Octave – Minor Sixth – Perfect Prime (Unison) –
Major Seventh

Bottom Staff:

Major Sixth – Minor Seventh – Major Third – Minor
Second

Solution to Exercise 6

1. Relative keys to:

 F sharp major – D sharp minor

B flat major – G minor

2. Major and minor keys for each key signature:

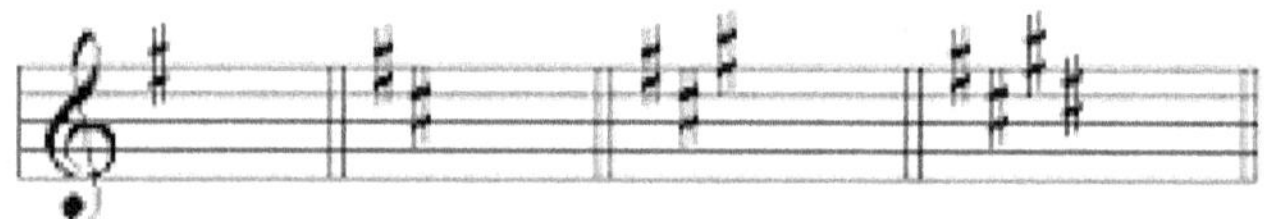

G Major – D Major – A Major – E Major

Solutions to Exercise 7

G minor 7th chord

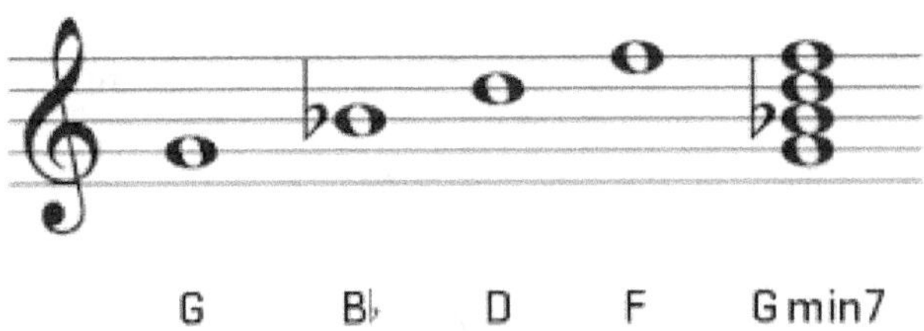

B-flat major 7th chord

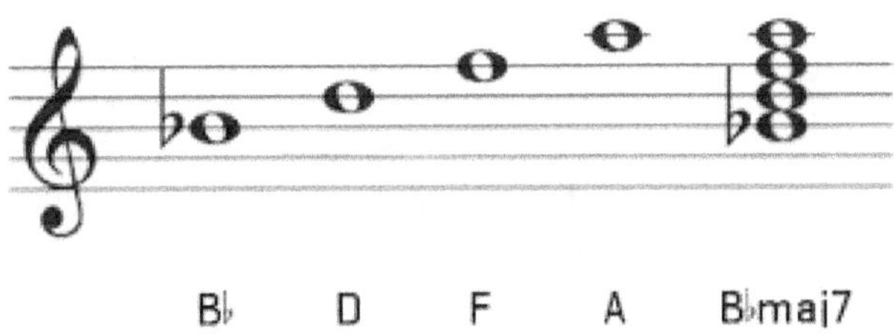

F-sharp minor 7th chord

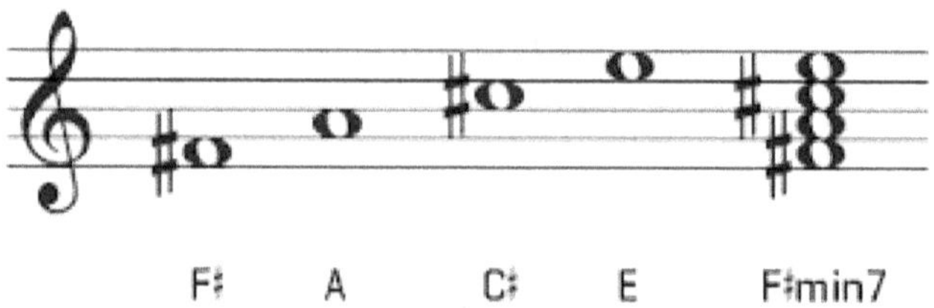

D diminished 7th chord

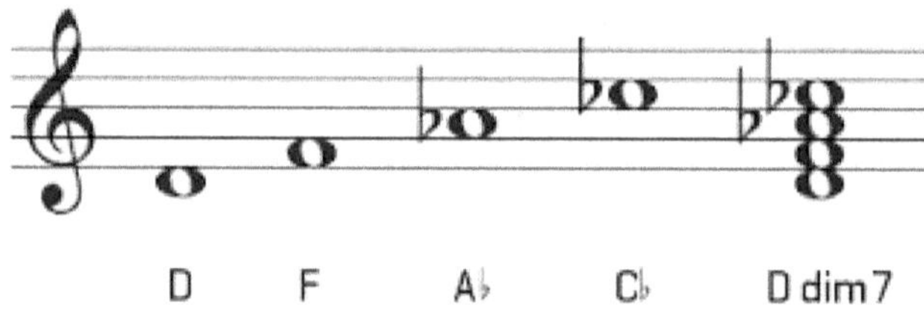

HOW TO READ
MUSIC
IN 1 DAY
The Only 7 Exercises You Need to Learn
Sheet Music Theory and Reading
Musical Notation Today
PRESTON HOFFMAN

BOOK 3

HOW TO READ MUSIC: IN 1 DAY

The Only 7 Exercises You Need to Learn Sheet Music Theory and Reading Musical Notation Today

Preston Hoffman

Table of Contents

Introduction 159

Chapter One: Fundamentals of Music Theory 161

Chapter Two: Fundamentals of Music Notation 186

Chapter Three: Elements of Reading Sheet Music 204

Chapter Four: Seven Step-by-Step Exercises to Help You Learn How to Read Sheet Music 209

Conclusion 214

Introduction

Music can be described as a chronological organization of sounds to create a beautiful form that is melodic, rhythmic and harmonious. Music has been a part of human culture long before recorded culture. It unifies the mind and soul and helps people express emotion. In the early days before the invention of audio recording and playback, people came up with a way of writing music as a way of communicating and preserving it. Written music is also referred to as sheet music. Written music language has been around for almost as long as the normal language we use to speak. It has undergone constant development through thousands of years. The written music language we use today has been around for over three decades.

Written music language is based on a system of notation that provides musicians with all the information they require to play a piece of music in the same way the composer intended it to be played. Music notation is a system that uses symbols to represent sounds and other aspects of music, such as timing, pitch, and duration. Music notation can also be used to represent more advanced aspects of music such as timbre, expression, and even special musical effects.

Learning how to read sheet music can be a bit of a challenging task, in particular for people who have not attended any prior music lessons. Like with learning most other skills, it is important to realize that there is no magic bullet for learning how to read music. However, with practice, anyone can learn how to read music, especially when it is broken down into small, simple steps.

This book will give you an introduction to the basics of reading music, give you a basic understanding of the fundamentals of music theory and notation and the elements of reading sheet music. It will also give you simple, step-by-step exercises that will help you learn how to read sheet music in one day.

Chapter One: Fundamentals of Music Theory

Before getting into sheet music and how it is written and read, it is important to have a very, very solid understanding of music theory. Music theory looks at various aural phenomena and how they are applied in music. It also considers the reasoning behind music – what makes music work as well as the rules followed by composers when creating music. Here are the basic aural phenomena that constitute the fundamentals of music.

Pitch

Pitch is a measure of how high or low a tone is. While pitch can be accurately measured, music theorists consider pitch to be subjective. This is because most natural sounds are comprised of a complex mix of several frequencies. In music, letter names are used to represent some specific frequencies. For instance, in most orchestras, the frequency of 440 HZ is referred to as the Concert A. However, this is not standard. There are no hard rules on how to assign letter names to different frequencies.

Most cultures allow pitch to vary in different pieces of music depending on mood, style, and genre. If you go back to France in the 1850's, the A represented 435 Hz. However, there is a specific convention that is followed. Pitches are assigned the first seven letters of the alphabet, from A all the way to G, with A representing the lowest pitch and G representing the highest pitch. Pitches higher than G start over again at A but with a higher octave. Pitches with the same name but different octaves are referred to as a pitch class. A frequency difference between two pitches is known as an interval.

Intervals

An interval refers to the distance between two pitches. Interval names consist of a number and a prefix. The number denotes the number of pitch names between the two pitches. For instance, there are two pitch names between the whole step F to G. These two pitch names are F and G. Since this interval has two pitches names, it is known as a second. However, the interval from F to A has three pitches; F, G and A. This interval is therefore known as a third. This goes on until we get to the pitch interval with eight pitch names. Intervals with eight pitch names (for instance, F to F or A to A) are known as octaves. Intervals between two notes of the exact same pitch are known as unisons.

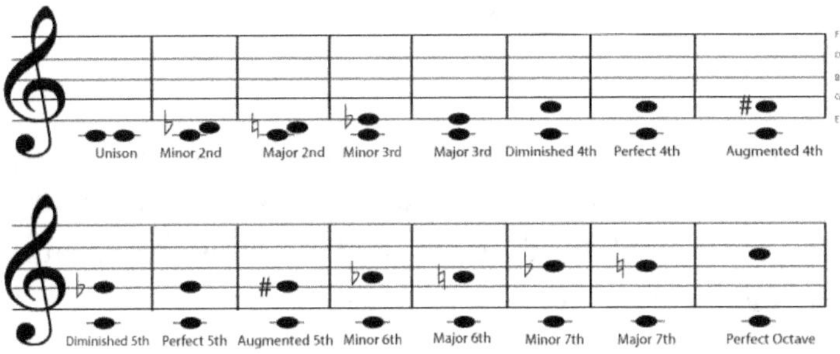

The different pitch intervals

The second part of an interval name is referred to as the prefix. The prefix is determined by the quality of the interval. There are five major prefixes that are used to describe intervals. A perfect interval is one that includes both an octave and a unison. Perfect intervals also have a fourth and a fifth. A perfect interval is labelled with the symbol 'P.' The next prefix is the major. This can only describe seconds, thirds, sixths and sevenths. A capital 'M' is used to label major intervals. Minor intervals are formed as a result of making a major interval smaller by half a step. This can be accomplished either by raising the bottom note by half a step or lowering the top note by half a step. A small 'm' is used to label a minor interval.

Another prefix that is commonly used to describe intervals is the augmented interval. This occurs when a major or perfect interval is made bigger by half a step without changing the interval number. Augmented intervals can be labeled using a capital 'A', the '+' symbol or the abbreviation 'Aug'. Finally, we have diminished intervals. These occur when a perfect or minor interval is made smaller by half a step, while maintaining its initial interval number. A small 'd', the abbreviations 'dim' or

163

'deg' or the symbol '°' can be used to denote a diminished interval.

From the above, it becomes evident that octaves, unisons, fourths and fifths can be either diminished, perfect or augmented. On the other hand, thirds, sixths and sevenths can be either diminished, augmented, major or minor.

Scales and Key Signatures

Musical notes are sometimes arranged in scales. A scale is a set of notes which are ordered per increasing or decreasing differences in pitch. The pitches in a scale span an octave. Scales that include both half and whole steps are known as diatonic scales. Each note within a diatonic scale has a specific name. The first and last notes in a diatonic scale are known as the tonic. Tonics are the easiest to find and the most stable. As a result, you will find that most diatonic melodies will often end with a diatonic note. The second note in the diatonic scale is known as the supertonic. The third note, which sits halfway between the tonic and the dominant is known as the mediant. After the mediant comes the subdominant, which is the fourth note in the diatonic scale. The fifth note is known as the dominant. Next to the dominant, we have the submediant. The seventh note is known as the subtonic. In the major, harmonic and melodic minor scales, if the seventh note is half a step lower than the tonic, it is referred to as the leading note.

The Major Scale

This is one of the most famous scales. This scale is made up of seven different pitches. The escalation of pitches on this scale is what is expressed by the familiar "Doh Re Mi Fa So La Ti Doh". The Major Scale has two half steps. One falls between the third and the fourth scale degrees while the other falls between the seventh and eighth scale degress. The other scale degrees are separated by whole steps. Below is an image of the C Major Scale.

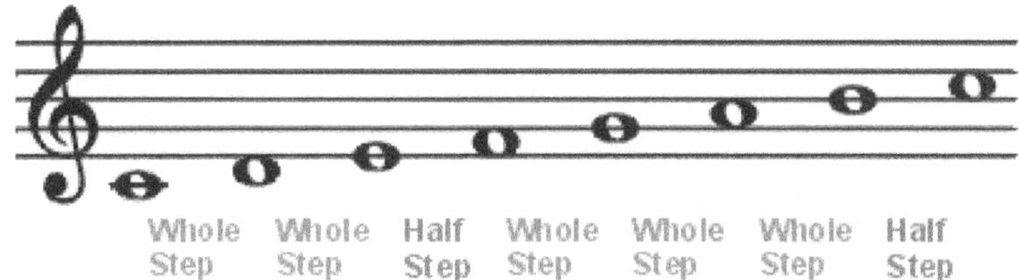

Whole and half steps in the C major scale

All major scales maintain the same pattern of whole and half steps. To construct another major scale, you only need to change the first note and then maintain the same sequence of whole and half steps.

The Natural Minor Scales

Natural minor scales consist of seven different scale degrees, with two half steps. The first half step falls between the second and third degree while the second falls between the fifth and sixth degree. The other scale degrees are separated by whole steps. Below is an image of the A minor scale. Just as with the major scales, you can construct other minor scales by changing the first note of the A minor scale and maintaining the same pattern.

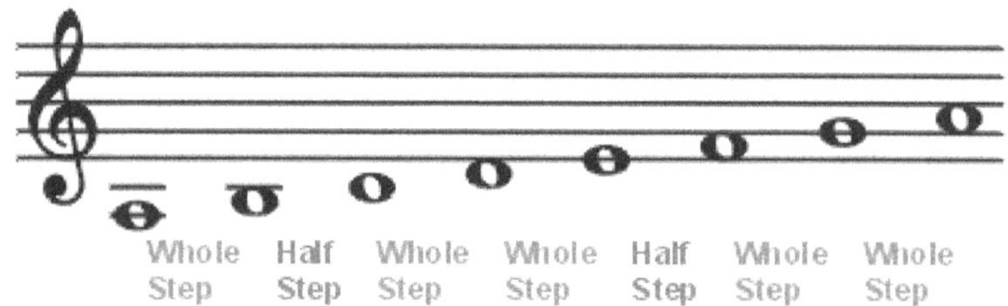

Whole and half steps in the A minor scale

The Harmonic Minor Scale

The Haromonic minor is similar to the natural minor scale. However, the seventh step of the harmonic minor scale is raised half a step. This means that the interval between the sixth and seventh notes becomes one and a half steps while the interval between the seventh and eighth notes becomes one half step. Below is an image of the harmonic A minor scale.

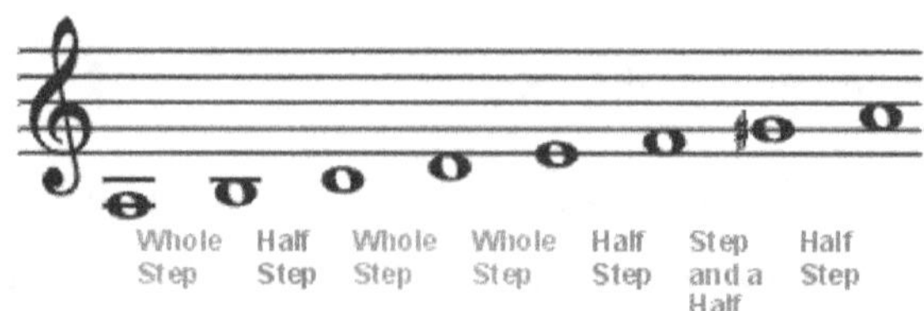

Whole, half and one and half steps in the harmonic minor scale

The Melodic Minor Scale

This is another scale that is the result of a slight variation of the natural minor scale. Here, the sixth and seventh notes are both raised by half a step. All the other notes maintain the same pattern as with the natural major scale. Below is an image of the melodic A minor scale.

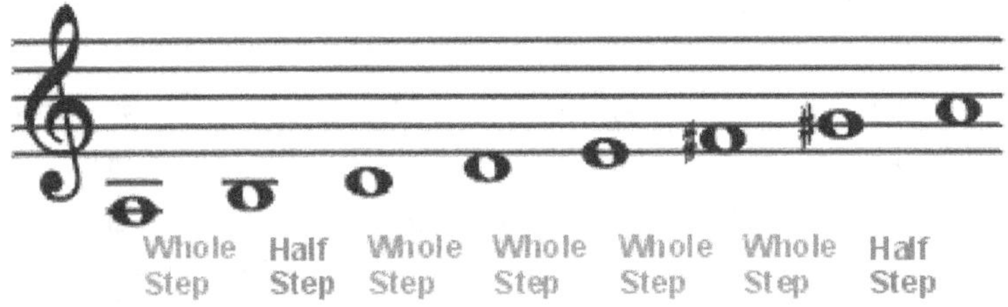

Whole and half steps on the melodic minor scale

Pentatonic Scales

As their name suggests, pentatonic scales consist of only five notes. Since they are a couple of notes less than the diatonic scales, pentatonic scales need intervals of more than half a step in order to get from one end of the scale to the other.

Some scales do not follow the interval sequences of either the diatonic or pentatonic scales. Such scales are known as nondiatonic scales. Most nondiatonic scales do not have an identifiable tonic.

An example of a well-known non-diatonic scale in Western music theory is the chromatic scale, which consists of an octave divided into twelve consecutive tones. This scale only consists of half steps. Since all the notes are equidistant, the chromatic scale does not have a tonic. Whole tone scales, on the other hand, are non-diatonic scales that are comprised of whole steps only. Whole tone scales also do not have tonics. The blues scale is another scale that is derived by adding a chromatic variation to the major scale. The blues scale has flat thirds and sevenths alternating with normal thirds and sevenths. The blues inflection occurs as a result of this alternation.

Transposition

It is possible to duplicate scale patterns at different pitches. This is known as transposition. For instance, if you write the major scale pattern but decide to start at the pitch G, the result becomes a transposition. However, you would still maintain the same pattern used by the major scale. It is possible to modify all the notes of a piece of music this way.

In some cases, however, some notes become sharp once they are transposed. In such instances, you might opt to place accidentals at the beginning of the piece. This modifies all the notes of a specific pitch. By placing the accidental at the beginning of the piece (instead of right beside the note), the accidental affects all the notes in the piece. For instance, placing a sharp at the beginning of line F makes all the Fs sharp. This designation of sharps and flats at the beginning of a piece is known as a key signature.

Key Signatures

In Western music theory, the pitches that make up a scale are designated by key signatures at the beginning of a composition. At times, the scale may shift as the music progresses. However, the interval relationships do not change even when the scale changes. To make key signatures easier to understand and remember, sometimes a chart known as the circle of fifths is used. On the outer side of this chart are the major key names. They are separated by fifths. On the inside of the chart are the minor key names. Between the two are staves showing the number and positions of the flats and sharps.

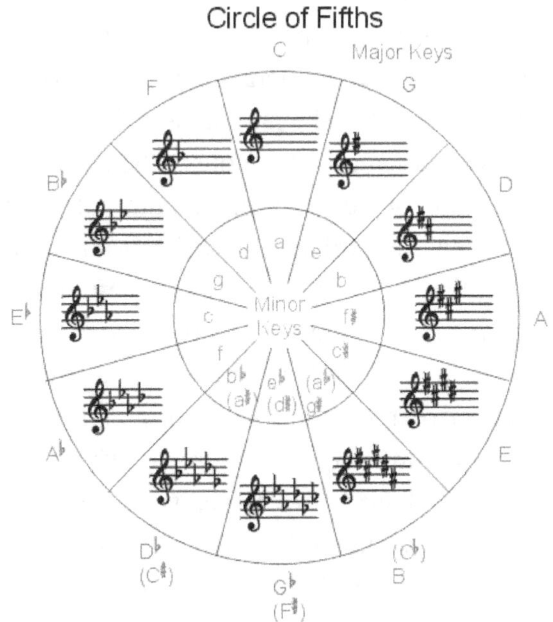

Modes

A mode refers to a type of scale that is coupled with specific melodic behaviors. Modes were developed in the middle ages as a way of organizing the melodic and harmonic parts of music. The usage of modes fell somewhat from the 17th to the 19th century. They were replaced by the major and minor scales. However, modes are still used in contemporary music. Unlike the tonic in a diatonic scale, the beginning tone of a mode is known as the final.

There are several modes. The most common is the Dorian mode, which resembles the natural minor scale with the sixth note raised. The half steps in the Dorian mode fall between the second and third and the sixth and seventh degrees. The Phrygian mode corresponds to the natural minor scale, with the second note lowered. The half steps fall between the first and second and fifth and sixth notes. The Lydian mode corresponds to the major scale, with a raised fourth note. The half steps fall between the fourth and fifth and seventh and eighth notes. The Mixolydian mode is similar to the major scale, with the seventh note lowered. The half steps fall between the third and fourth and sixth and seventh notes. The Aeolian mode is similar to the natural minor scale. Its half steps are placed between the second and third and fifth and sixth notes. The Ionian mode is similar to the major scale, with the half steps between the third and fourth and seventh and eighth notes. Finally, we have the Locrian mode, which corresponds to the natural minor, albeit with lowered second and fifth notes. The half steps on the Locrian mode fall between the first and second and fourth and fifth notes. However, Locrian modes are rarely used.

Just like scales, modes can begin on any tone, provided that the pattern of half and whole steps remains unchanged.

Identifying the identity of a transposed mode is easy since its final lies in the same position as the tonic of a major with a similar key signature.

Solfeggio

Solfeggio, sometimes referred to as solfege is a voice exercise which is used to teach pitch and sight singing. The solfeggio consists of syllables which are associated to specific notes in each scale. The syllable 'Do' corresponds to the first note or the tonic. The next syllable is 'Re', which corresponds to the supertonic. The mediant is represented by the syllable 'Mi'. The subdominant is represented by the syllable 'Fa'. The dominant is represented by the syllable 'Sol'. The next syllable is 'La', which represents the submediant. Finally, we have the syllable 'Ti', which corresponds to the leading tone.

Consonance and Dissonance

This refers to the categorization of sounds that are played simultaneously or successively. Consonant notes sound pleasant, sweet and stable when played together. Dissonant notes sound unpleasant or harsh. It is important to note that consonance and dissonance are subjective. What sounds good to one person may not sound pleasant to the other. These values may also be affected by context and other aspects such as tuning. However, there are common notes that are associated with consonance or dissonance.

Consonance and dissonance applies to both intervals and chords. The octave, the major and minor third, the perfect fourth and fifth and the major and minor sixth are simple intervals that are associated with consonance. They sound pleasing when played together.

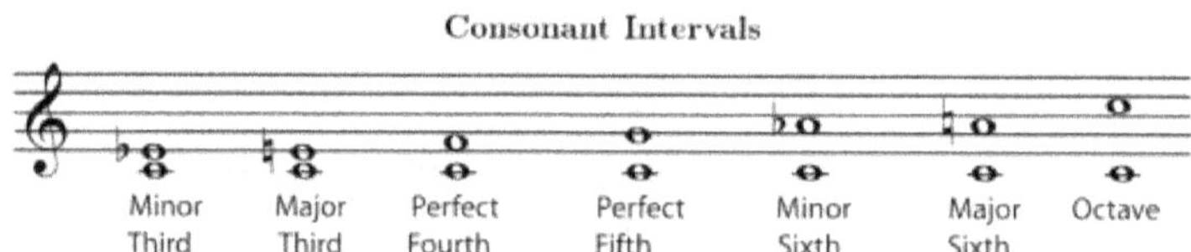

The major and minor second, the major and minor seventh and triton (the interval between the perfect fourth and fifth) are intervals associated with dissonance. They seem to clash when played together. When we hear dissonant chords, we expect them to move to a consonant chord. When a dissonance moves to a consonance, this is known as a resolution. A good pattern of dissonances and consonances is what makes music exciting.

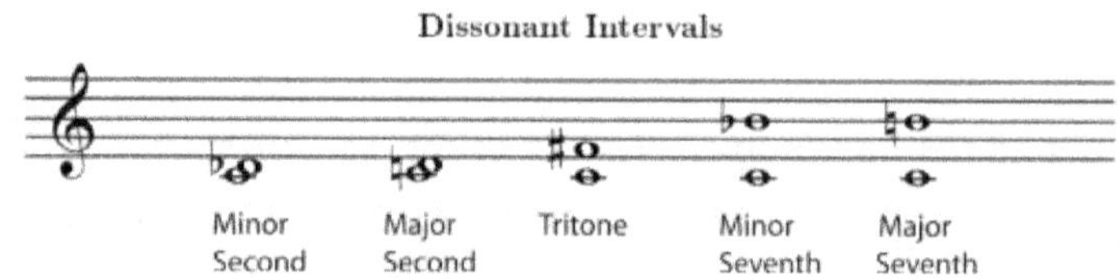

Rhythm

Rhythm in a piece of music refers to the sequential arrangement of sounds and silences as they progress through time. Rhythm can also be referred to as the basic pulse or pattern that is repeated through the progress of a piece of music. These pulses are referred to as beats. In a written piece of music, the beats are placed together in groupings known as measures or bars. In most pieces of music, the bars have an equal number of beats. The first beat in a bar usually sounds as the strongest. The bars in a piece of music set up the underlying rhythm of the music.

Melody

This is one of the foundational elements of music theory. A melody is a series of notes of a particular pitch and duration, stringed together to form a succession that typically escalates towards a crescendo of tension before resolving to a state of rest. However, a melody is more than a series of notes. A melody is the part of music that catches your ear. The basic elements that comprise a melody are the pitch, rhythm, duration and tempo of the string of notes.

There are some other important terms that are used to describe melody. The series of notes that make up a melody are known as the melodic line. Ornaments or embellishments refer to notes that the composer or performer adds to make a melody exciting and complex. They are not part of the main melodic line. They only serve to enhance the melody.

Melody affects how music sounds. A melody usually involves changes in pitch as it progresses to keep the music interesting. A melody that progresses on one pitch will quickly become boring. The rise and fall of the pitch of a melody written on the staff creates a line that rises and falls. This line is referred to as the shape or contour of the melodic line.

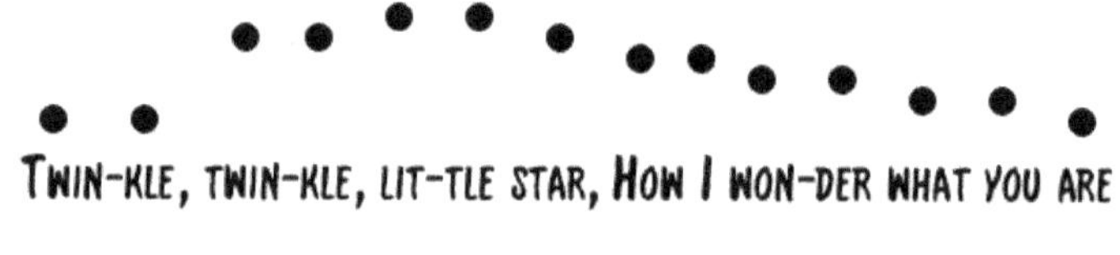

Melodic contour of a popular musical composition

Chord

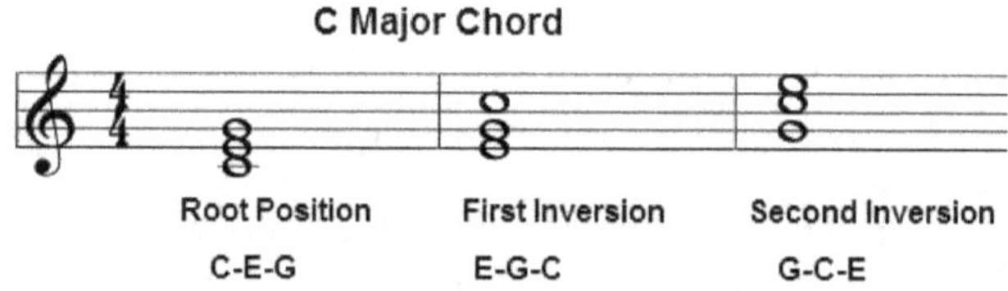

In music theory, a chord is a set of three or more harmonic notes that sound as if they are played simultaneously. They don't need to actually be played together. Chords and sequences of chords (ordered sequences of chords, also known as chord progressions) are common in most kinds of modern Western,

Oceanian and West African music. However, they are lacking in music from most other parts of the world.

The most common kind of chords are known as triads. Triads are made up of three distinct notes – the root note and two intervals of a third and fifth directly on top of the root note. More notes can be added to triads to form other kinds of chords like the extended chords, seventh cords or added tone chords. The most common chords include the minor and major triads and the augmented and diminished triads. The phrases minor, major, diminished and augmented are sometimes used to refer to the quality of the chord. The root note is usually used to classify chords. For instance, a major chord that is rooted on the note C is classified as chord C major.

Harmony

Harmony is another one of the key tenets of music theory. Harmony occurs in music when more than one pitches, tones, notes or chords are sounded at the same time. Harmony refers to how the tones and chords accompanying a melody interplay together to add meaning and depth to music. In music, harmony does have to actually sound "harmonious". The essence of harmony of the notes, pitches and chords sounding simultaneously. In some cases, harmony may actually be dissonant.

Harmonies in music come in different textures. When a melody is composed such that it strongly suggests a harmony that could go together with it – even without any other notes sounding simultaneously – is known as **implied harmony**. The easiest way of adding harmony to a melody is by playing it alongside **drones**. These are notes that do not change throughout the course of a musical piece. When different lines in a piece of music rise and fall together in accordance with the melody, this is known as **parallel harmony**. When a piece of music has one distinct melodic line while the rest of the notes are included simply to add harmony, this is known as **homophony**. When a piece of music has more than one independent and fairly equal melodic lines, this is known as **polyphony** or a **counterpoint**.

Timbre

Sometimes referred to as "color", this refers to the differences in musical sound resulting from the instrument used to play the sound. This is what enables us to distinguish between two different instruments. For instance, if a flute and recorder play the same note at the same pitch and volume, you can distinguish between the sounds from the two instruments. This difference between the two sounds is what is known as timbre.

The differences in timber between different instruments arises from the fact that each instrument produces sounds in a complex wave that has more than one frequency. As humans, we do not hear these different frequencies as separate notes. Instead, we hear them as a mixture of frequencies that form the color of the sound. In addition, the timbre of an instrument can be altered by employing different playing techniques.

Humans are capable of perceiving and appreciating very minute differences in the timbre of musical sounds. Not only can a person tell the difference between two instruments, they can also distinguish between two instruments of the same kind.

There are many different words used to describe various forms of timbre. Some of these words are interchangeable and have no specific definitions. Some of these include dull, clear, bright, rounded, harsh, mellow, warm, reedy, dark, shrill, piercing, brassy, strident, and so on.

Dynamics

In music, dynamics refers to how loud or quiet a performance is. While the volume of a musical performance can be accurately measured by audio engineers, dynamics are not given any absolute values in music notation. Instead, dynamics are considered as relative values. Since dynamics are a subjective value, the volume of a performance is determined by several factors aside from amplitude, including factors like timer and articulation.

In a written piece of music, dynamics are represented by symbols or abbreviations which show the volume at which different notes should be played. These symbols are derived from the Italian language and are used to indicate the different parts that require different volumes in the same way punctuation is used in a sentence.

Below are some of the symbols used to represent various levels intensity, together with their actual Italian and English meanings.

Abbreviation	Italian word	English meaning
ppp	Pianississamo	Very, very quiet
pp	Pianissimo	Very quiet
mp	Mezzopiano	Quite quiet
p	Piano	Quiet
f	Forte	Loud
mf	Mezzoforte	Quite loud
ff	Fortissimo	Very loud
fff	Fortississimo	Very, very loud
sf	Sforzando	Suddenly very loud
cres.	Cresendo	Getting louder
dim.	Diminuendo	Getting quieter

Articulation

In music, articulation refers to the performer's style and how it impacts the length or duration of a series of notes in relation to each other. Articulation is not quantified. Instead, it is only described, giving the performer room to interpret how to execute the articulation. Articulation marks are used to express articulations. These articulation marks establish a relationship between the notes in a piece of music and modify their execution.

Some common articulation marks used in music include the staccato, staccatissimo, marcato, legato, slur, detache, rinforzando and sforzando. There are symbols that are used above articulation marks to specify the type of articulation. For instance, a dot is used to indicate a staccato while a curved line connecting two or more notes indicates a slur.

Most types of articulations can be fitted into one of three general categories. Some articulations represent **dynamic change**. These show the need for a change in volume in relation to surrounding notes. The sforzando and marcato are examples of articulations that represent dynamic change. Articulations like the tenuto, staccato and staccatissimo represent **length change**. They are used to elongate or shorten notes. While every articulation changes a note in relation to the notes around it, some articulations affect a group of notes as a whole. These articulations represent **relationship change**. Examples of articulations that represent relationship change are the slur and detache.

Texture

The texture of a piece of music refers to how the composer combines the melody, rhythm and harmony to bring out the general quality of the piece. Put simply, texture describes how complex a musical composition is, or how different layers or elements are used in the piece to create a musical "tapestry." Texture is very often a relative term, though it can also be distinguished specifically depending on the number of elements in the compositions and how they relate to each other. Texture is affected by tempo, harmony and rhythm of a piece, the amount and richness of instruments used to play the piece as well as the timbre of these instruments.

The following terms are commonly used to describe texture:

Monophonic: This is a composition has a single melodic line. There's no harmony or counterpoint.

Biphonic: Biphonic music has two different melodies that play simultaneously.

Heterophonic: Consists of a single melody, with different variations of this melody being played or sung simultaneously.

Homophonic: Music that has a single melodic line with chords or accompaniment.

Polyphonic: This is a piece of music that has several harmonies and voices.

Form or Structure

Form refers to the overall plan or structure of a piece of music. In other words, form looks at the big picture in a piece of music. There is a great range of complexity in musical form. While most listeners will quickly understand the form of short, simple pieces of music, it can be difficult to understand the form of more complex or unfamiliar types of music. A person can still enjoy a piece of music without having to recognize its form. However, seeing the "big picture" makes the music even more enjoyable for the listener.

Musical form can be described by labelling it with letters or giving names to the very common forms. For instance, the first major section in the piece of music can be labelled A. If another section is exactly similar to the first section, it also gets labelled A. If it is quite similar but has some distinct differences, it could be labelled A' (A prime). Another distinct variation of A could be labelled A" (A double prime).

Expression

Musical expression refers to the art of expressing emotion through music and invoking emotions from the audience. Expression thus forms an emotional link between the performer and the audience. Musical expression explores how a performer brings a piece of music to life through the appropriate use of dynamics, articulation, phrasing, intensity, timbre, energy and excitement. The aim of musical expression is to elicit responses from the audience. Through a piece of music, the performer can calm or excite the audience and affect their physical and emotional responses in other ways.

Musical expression is not the result of a single element. Instead, it is the result of a combination of several musical elements used simultaneously. Musical expression also depends on the natural ability of the performer to express deep emotions and sentiment.

Notation

Musical notation refers to the symbolized or written representation of a piece of music. Music is represented in written form through the use of generally accepted graphic symbols as well as written instructions and their abbreviations. Different cultures and different ages use different systems of music notation. The Western notation in use today evolved during the middle ages. To this day, it is still undergoing various forms of experimentation and innovation. Sometimes, hand signs and spoken language can also be used to represent music. However, these are mostly used in teaching.

Western music notation uses symbols (notes) placed on a musical staff to graphically represent tones. There are different symbols for representing other musical elements like dynamics, articulations. Duration, keys, rests, accents, etc. The conductor usually uses verbal instructions to indicate aspects like technique and tempo.

Common Practice Part Writing

Common-practice part writing is a very crucial skill in music theory. While modern musical law does not incorporate practice-writing, knowing the rules on which practice writing is based can be very advantageous in analyzing and understanding music. Common practice has its foundations on the rules of counterpoint. This is a set of rules which were very popular in the 18th and 19th centuries. The aim of counterpoint was to come up with harmonies and progressions that people from that era found enjoyable and acceptable. Counterpoint was used by famous musicians like Beethoven, Brahms, Mozart, Handel and Bach. Music written in this style is often divided into two parts, each with four different species: 1st, 2nd, 3rd and 4th. Each of these parts defines a different way that the part interacts with different rhythms.

Common practice part writing is best represented in four-part writing, the most common of which is the chorale style which uses two voice parts per clef. The chorale style is based around bass, tenor, alto and soprano voices. The tenor and bass voices are written on the bass clef while the soprano and alto voices are written on the treble clef. The four different voices are then used together to come up with chordal progressions. There are several different rules which are used to define the movement of chordal progressions.

When writing a piece of music, the composer must concentrate on the spacing and range of each instrument or voice. It is very important for the composer not to stretch the range of an instrument higher or lower than it is usually used to. They must also be very careful of spacing, since wrong spacing can lead to voice crossing. This is where a voice or instrument goes higher or lower than the voice that is above or below it. Common-practice part writing strictly forbids voice crossing. For instance, the soprano voice is not supposed to go lower than the alto voice.

When part writing, it is important to use the Conjunct Melodic Motion, where the different parts generally move in stepwise motion. If you are using counterpoint, if a part jumps to a fourth or above, it should then progress in stepwise motion in the direction opposite the jump. The different voices are also required to progress together in contrary motion, which means that each voice goes in a different direction. This is preferable to having the voices move together in parallel motion, or having one voice move while the other doesn't, as in oblique motion.

In cases where the composer decides to use parallel motion, they must pay special attention to the intervals to ensure that they are in line with the counterpoint rules. Dissonant intervals should be avoided, whether they are melodic or harmonic. This includes seventh chords, tritons and diminished or augmented intervals. Using these intervals results in a jarring piece of music. The composer should also be aware of parallel intervals. These occur when two voices move the same distance, resulting in a similar interval twice in a row. However, this is not always a problem, unless the intervals are a perfect octave or perfect fifth, in which case the piece has a hollow or open sound which is a bit uncomfortable to the ear.

Chapter Two: Fundamentals of Music Notation

People invented language long before they learned how to write. Similarly, people started making music long before they came up with a system of writing down music. Before the advent of written music, people played music by the ear. To this day, some musicians still play music this way. However, written music has a number of advantages. It is much easier to study and share. Written music also makes it possible for bands and large groups of musicians to play long, complex pieces exactly as the composer intended. While there are many different types of music notation in existence, the most common and most popular is the use of the staff.

The Staff

The staff (plural staves) is the backbone of written music. It provides a backdrop on which musical symbols are placed. The staff is made up of five horizontal parallel lines and the four spaces between them. Below is an image of a simple unadorned staff.

Musical notations are placed on the staff, either on the lines or in the spaces between them. The notation of music on the staff is very logical. The higher a note is on the staff, the higher the pitch of the note. The lower the note on the staff, the lower the pitch. Sometimes, a note may have an extreme pitch that goes beyond the staff, either too high or too low. In this case, ledger lines are used to temporarily extend the staff vertically to accommodate these notes. You can think of a staff like the two dimensional mathematical plane, with the Y-axis representing pitch while the X-axis represents time.

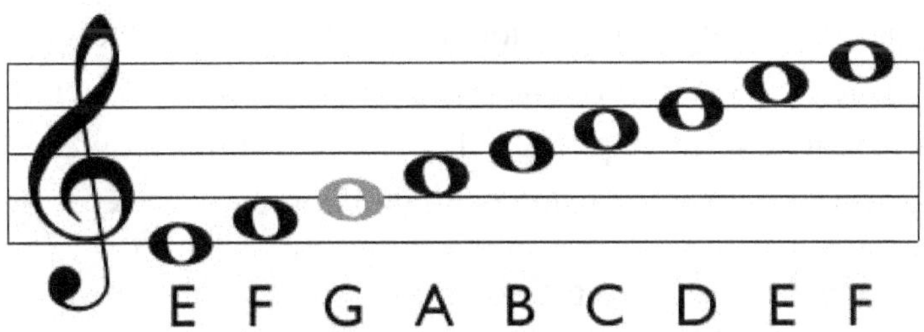

Staff adorned with notes

The notes and rests appearing on the staff are the actual written music. Notes represent sounds while rests represent silence. Vertical lines known as bar lines are used to divide the staff into short sections referred to as bars or measures, while double bar lines are used to signify the end of larger sections or even the end of a piece of music. Important symbols like clefs and time and key and time signatures are placed at the beginning of the staff. Other symbols are placed above the music to direct how other elements of the music should be executed.

Evolution of Staff Notation

The notation of musical notes and symbols on the modern staff evolved from the neumatic notations which was used between the 9th and 12th centuries for secular song and plainchant. Neumes were graphical symbols which were essentially used to indicate the rise and fall of the voice. Neumes themselves evolved from Greek and Roman symbols which were used to guide declamation. Different regions had different musical adaptations of these symbols. Unlike modern musical symbols, each neume consisted of two or more notes, with indications of their approximate relative pitches. The notes within a single syllable of text were represented using a single neume.

Unlike modern staff notation, neumes only acted as memory aids to singers who already knew a piece of music by heart. A singer who had no prior knowledge of the words and melody of a piece and music could not sing it by reading neumes. However, between the 10th and 12th centuries, there were significant developments towards a notation system that could allow people to sight-read music. 'Distematic' neumes, also known as 'heighted' neumes were used with varying spaces relative to each other, forming a continuous graph of pitch above the words of a piece of music.

Eventually, to make the pitch more precise, people started spacing the neumes on a horizontal grid of scratched lines. The degrees of a scale would then fall alternatively on a line or space in similar fashion to the modern staff. One line on the grid was colored red to represent the pitch F and another was colored yellow to represent pitch C. Eventually, the letters F or C started being used at the beginning of the appropriate lines to represent these pitches. By the 13th century, a four line staff was widely in use, with stylized forms of the letters F, C and G acting as clefs. By the 14th century, the five line staff had become the standard for polyphonic music.

In the 12th century, musicians in northern and north eastern France started adding more thickness to the thin, curved lines of neumes at specific points to define the separate notes within the neumes. This led to the rise of groupings of notes known as ligatures. Later, the ligatures were used to represent polyphonies which were without text. No longer tied to syllabic considerations, the ligatures attained rhythmic significance. However, the meaning of the ligatures still depending on context. In the 13th century, time values were codified for the ligatures, single notes and rests.

These new symbols with codified time values would form the basis for the mensural notation, which was popular between the 13th to 15th centuries. In the mensural notation system, the value of a note was determined relative to the value of its neighbors, based on several fundamental principles that were the basis of this system. This system would later evolve into the modern staff notation beginning in the 16th century. Longer note values became obsolete and shorter ones were introduced. The use of bar lines to measure meter, which had started in the late 15th century, became part of staff notation in the 17th century. Other aspects like regularly spaced barring and separate tempo indications become part of staff notation in the 18th and 19th centuries.

Groups of Staves

Just like normal text, music on the staff is read from left to right. Therefore, the notes to the left are played before those to the right. From the top of the page, each staff is read on its own, unless there is a group of connected staff. Connected staves should be played simultaneously. They are usually connected by a long vertical line on the left hand side. In other cases, bar lines may be used to connect staves. If a group of staves should be played by similar instruments or the same person, braces or brackets are used to group these staves together.

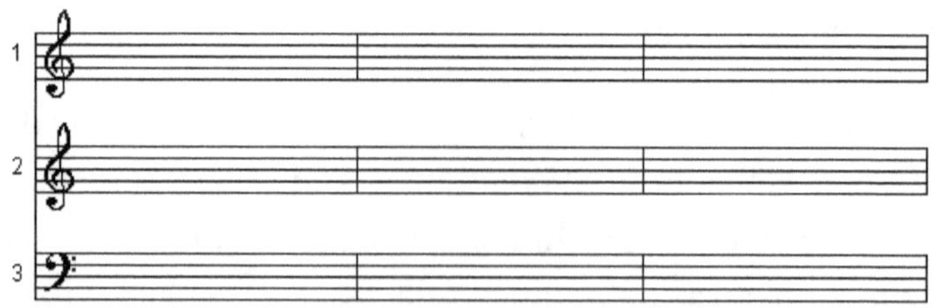

The Grand Staff

The grand staff is a combination of the bass and treble clef, connected together by a brace and line. This allows for notation of a wide range of pitches. The grand staff is commonly used in playing piano music, since it can accommodate the piano's wide range. It tells exactly which key should be played when.

Clefs

Clefs are the fancy symbols that appear at the beginning of each music staff. The clef symbol is used to associate the lines and spaces of the staff with particular pitches. There are many clefs in existence, many of which were used in the past. Today, only a couple of clefs are still used regularly. These are:

The Treble Clef

The treble clef, also known as the G-clef, is the most common clef in written music. It marks a treble sound. The treble clef, which is shaped like a stylized G, coils around the second the second lowermost line on the staff. It marks this line to be a G. From that, one can come up with the arrangement of the next letters on the staff. Each next letter is placed on a higher space or line. You should also note that the letter G is followed by an A. The lines on a treble staff in ascending order are E, G, B, D, F. You can use the following mnemonic to remember them: Every Good Boy Deserves Fudge. The spaces in ascending order are F, A, C, E, spelling the word FACE.

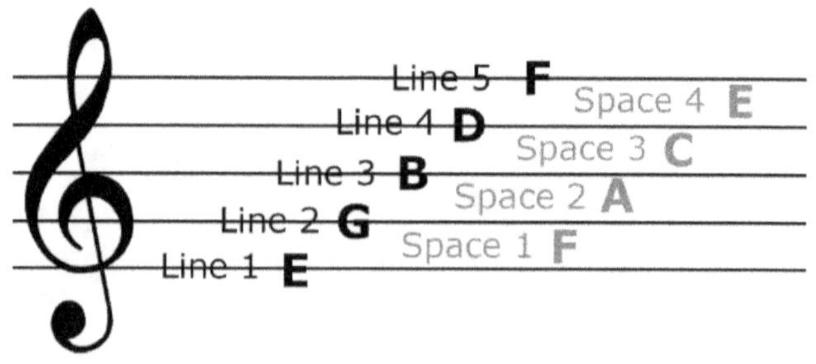

The Bass Clef

The bass clef is also known as the F clef. This clef designates the note F as the line bracketed by the two dots on the F-clef symbol. From there, one can identify the rest of the notes, which are still arranged in ascending order. This F-clef staff is usually used for low-pitched instruments. The lines on the bass staff, in ascending order are G, B, D, F, A. To remember the names of the lines on a bass staff, use the mnemonic "Good Boys Don't Fool Around". The spaces on this staff are A, C, E, and G. The spaces can be remembered using the following mnemonic: All Cows Eat Grass.

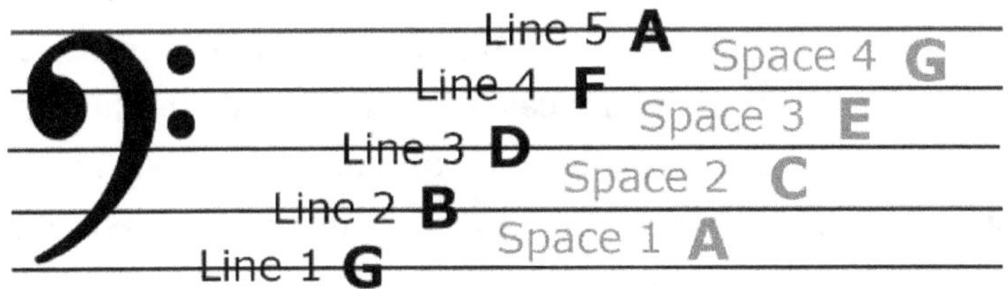

The C-Clef

Another clef that was popular is the C-clef, though its use is very infrequent nowadays. The C-clef is a movable clef. It can be placed anywhere on the staff. It has different names depending on its position on the staff. Depending on what line it is on, it is given names like the Alto Clef, the Tenor Clef, the Baritone Clef, the Soprano Clef or the Mezzo Soprano Clef. Regardless of its position, the line on which the C-Clef centers represents a middle C.

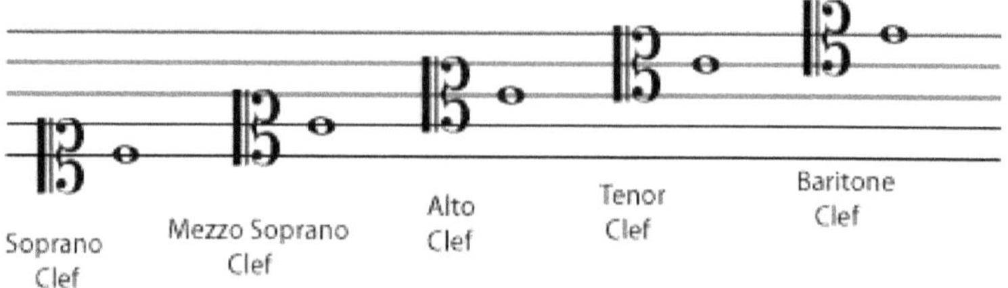

Measures

Measures, also known as bars, are marked by the vertical lines on the staff. They are used to organize music into sections. The number of beats in a measure is determined by the time signature. The beginning and end of a piece of music are marked using thick double bars. Sometimes, numbers are used to mark measures for easier navigation.

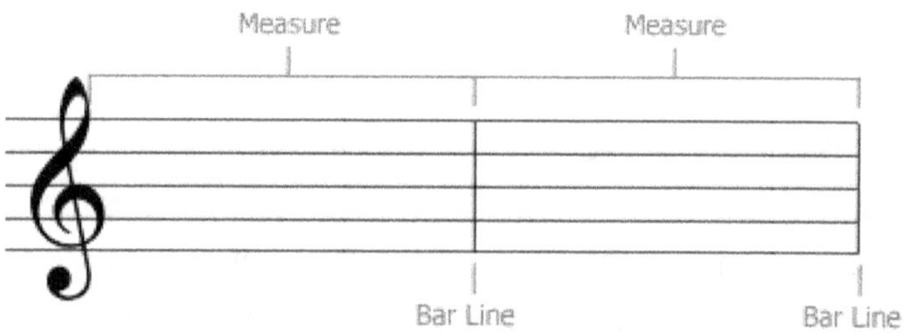

Notes

Notes are used to represent pitches on the staff, with letters being used to distinguish between the different pitches. The letters used to name pitches, in ascending order, are A, B, C, D, E, E, F and G. After G, the cycle starts again at A. The different lines of the staff represent different pitches, with lower lines representing low pitches and higher lines representing higher pitches. A note is represented on the staff using a small oval symbol.

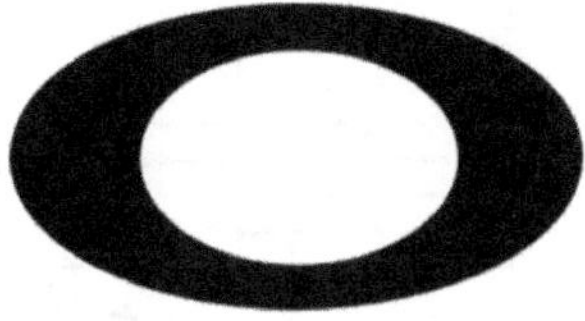

Notes on the Staff

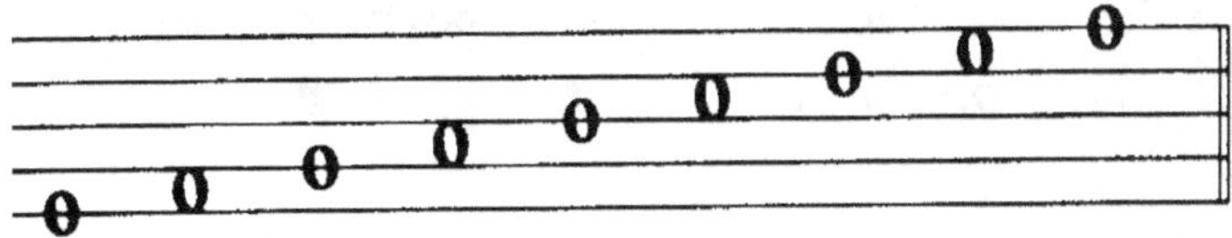

Notes are either placed on the lines or within the spaces on the staff. For notes with stems, the stems are placed on the left side of the note trailing down if the note is above the middle line. For those below the middle line, the stem rises upwards from the right side of the note. For notes on the middle line, the stem usually goes down, unless there are adjacent notes with flags that go up. The stems are usually one octave long (4 lines and 4 spaces). In case there are two melodies on the same staff, the stems for notes of one melody point up while those of the other melody point down.

Ledger Lines

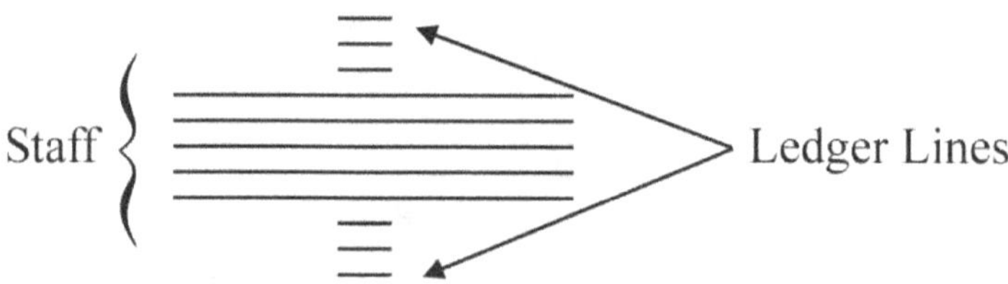

Ledger lines are lines that extend the vertical length of the staff, allowing for notes with higher or lower pitches than the staff to still be shown on the staff. The naming of ledger lines follows the same pattern used for the lines of the staff. The stems of notes placed on ledger lines point towards the center of the staff.

Note Durations

Each note has a specific duration.

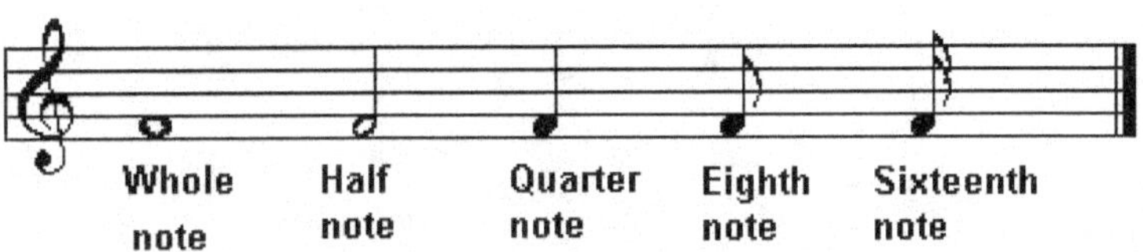

The largest note value is the whole note. A whole note has double the duration of a half note. Similarly, a half note has double the length of a quarter note, while a quarter note has double the length of an eighth note. An eighth note has double the length of a sixteenth note. This hierarchy can continue to infinity, with an addition of flags as the note is broken down into smaller units.

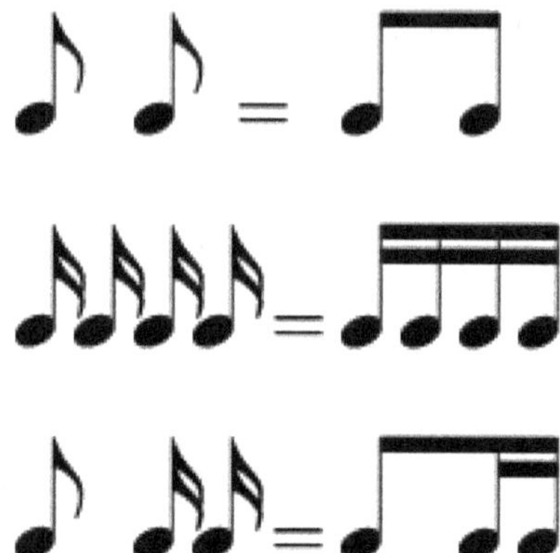

Two sixteenth or eighth notes can also be combined to look like the above image. Since eighth and sixteenth notes have flags, when they combine the flags are turned into connecting bars. An eighth and a sixteenth may also be combined.

Dotted Notes

Dots may be used besides notes. They increase the length of a note by half its original length. For instance, if a half note was worth 2 beats, placing a dot next to it makes it worth three beats.

Rests

Rests are periods of silence where the musician does not play any note. Rests are given values that correspond to those of notes. Therefore, just like notes, there are whole rests, half rests, quarter rests and so on. Unlike notes which change their vertical position depending on the pitch, rests always maintain the same vertical position.

Accidentals

Accidentals are used to modify the pitch of a note. They do this by either decreasing or increasing the pitch by half a step. Once an accidental appears on the staff, it affects all the notes of equivalent pitch for the remaining part of the measure. However, when they appear at the very beginning of a piece of music, accidentals are used to specify key signature.

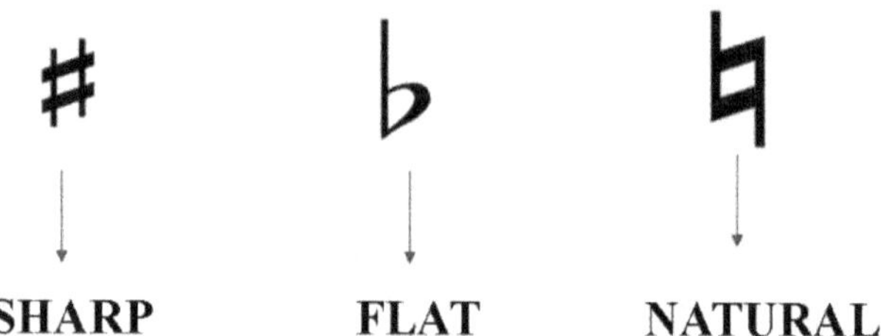

There are three types of accidental symbols. Flats are used to take the pitch of a note a half step lower. Sharps are used to raise the pitch of a note a half step higher, while naturals cancel out any previous accidentals. When a natural appears, the pitch goes back to normal.

Ties and Slurs

Ties and slurs are used to link together two or more notes. Ties link together notes of the same pitch to create a single but longer note. Slurs, on the other hand, link together notes of different pitches. In effect, this means that these notes should be played without any break between them.

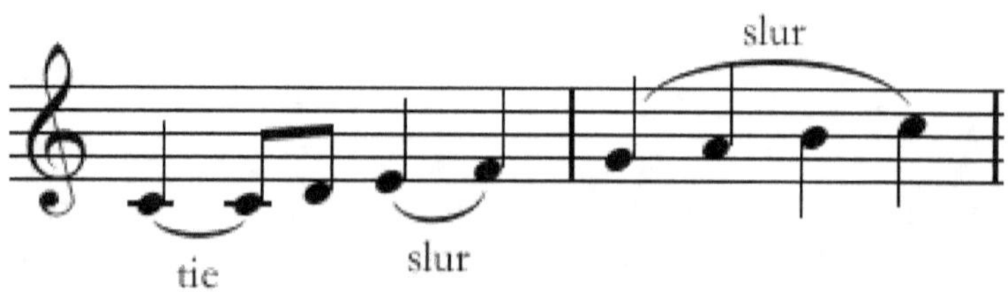

Repeats

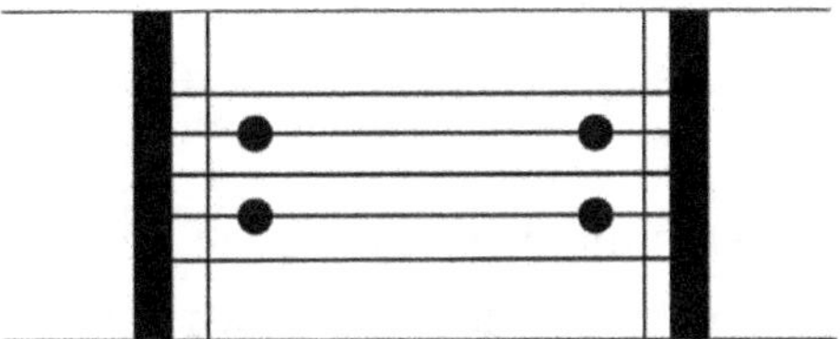

The above symbols are used to show the beginning and end of a repeat. When you come across the second repeat sign, it means that you should go back and repeat the music from the point where the first repeat sign appeared. Repeat signs usually go hand in hand with endings.

$$D.S.$$

This stands for 'Del Signo'. It is a directional marking. When this appears in a piece of music, it directs the player to go to the sign (Shown below). The Del Signo symbol usually goes hand in hand with an 'al coda' or al fine'. When accompanied by 'al coda', it means that you should 'Go to the sign, from there go to the coda'. If accompanied by an 'al fine', it means 'Go to the sign, from there go to the end'.

This is the sign that was referred to above. From here, the music should be plated to the coda or wherever the Del Signo indicates.

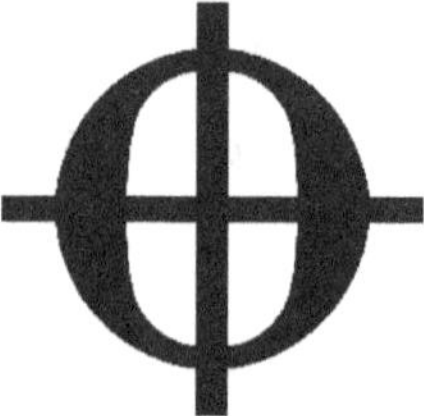

The above sign represents the coda. It shows instances where the player is supposed to go to the special ending, also known as the coda.

Time Signatures

These are also known as meter signatures. They tell the player the number of beats in a measure and the notes that get the beat.

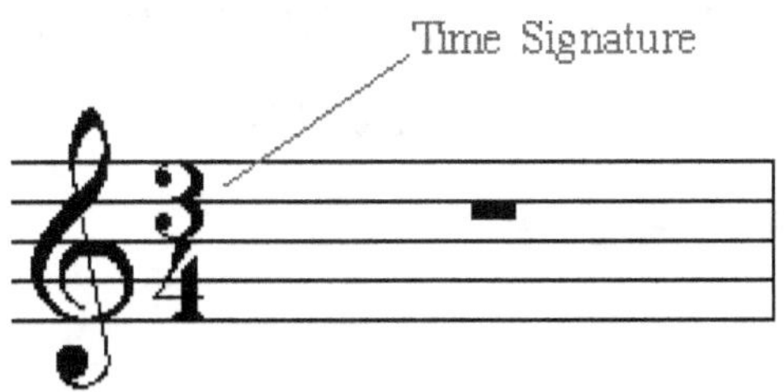

The top number in the time signature shows the number of beats in the measure. The bottom number, on the other hand, determines the note that gets the beat. For instance, when the time signature is 3/4, it means that each measure has 3 beats, while the beat goes to the fourth note.

Chapter Three: Elements of Reading Sheet Music

Sheet music refers to music where the different musical aspects of the composition – pitches, chords, rhythms, melodies, etc. – are represented in handwritten or printed form using modern musical symbols placed on a staff. Sheet music has different parts, comes in different types and is written for different purposes and uses.

Title And Credit

The first thing in a piece of music is the title of the song or composition. In most modern forms of sheet music, the title of the composition is indicated on the cover or title page. If there is no cover or title page, the title is indicated at the top of the first page. If the composition or song is taken from a bigger work such as a movie or opera, the title of the main work is also indicated. The name of the songwriter or composer is usually written along with the title of the composition. If the songwriter is unknown, this can be left out. If the lyrics of the song are written by a different person, the name of the lyric-writer may also be included. This is the same case for the name of the arranger. If the composition is an old folk music, a traditional hymn or spiritual or if it belongs to traditional genres such as blues, the name of the composer or songwriter is usually left out. This is because most of these songs have no known authors. For such pieces, the word "Traditional" is often used instead of the composer's name.

After the title and credit comes the actual written music, the elements of which were discussed in detail in the previous chapter.

Purpose and Use of Sheet Music

Sheet music is written for one of the following three reasons:

- To act as a record of music
- To act as a guide to a piece of music
- To provide the means for performing a piece of music.

To understand sheet music, one needs to be able to read music notation, which we discussed earlier. However, one does not need to be able to read or write music in order to compose music. Several famous songwriters and composers – the likes of Paul McCartney, John Stanley and Lionel Bert – have produced great music without being able to read music.

A popular skill when it comes to reading sheet music is sight reading. This is the ability of a person to perform a piece of music after viewing it for the first time, without prior practice. Most professional musicians are expected to be well skilled in sight reading. Some more experienced musicians can even hear all the sounds in a piece of music in their head after looking at it for the first time, without even having to hear the piece being played.

Sheet music is very important when it comes to performing some forms of music, such as chamber music, orchestral works, singing choral works and sonatas. The musicians performing these kinds of music usually have the sheet music on a music stand in front of them. However, musicians performing solo pieces do not usually read from sheet music. Instead, they are expected to memorize the music. Jazz music also uses an improvised form of sheet music known as a lead sheet to give indications of the different elements of the music.

Traditional forms of music rarely depend on sheet music. Instead, traditional musicians usually learn how to play music by the ear, or by being taught by another person. While sheet music often serves as a platform for new music and helps in the composition of new music, it can also act as a visual record of existing music.

Types of Sheet Music

Written music comes in different types. If a composition is meant to be played using only one instrument or voice, it is usually written as a single piece of sheet music. In other cases, a piece may be intended to be performed by different persons. In this case, each performer will have a different piece of the sheet music, which is known as a part.

Sometimes, separate vocal and instrumental parts of a piece of music may be written together, resulting in what is known as a score. There are various formats of musical scores:

Full score: This refers to a large book that shows the parts of the instruments and voices in a piece of music. Full scores are mainly used by conductors to lead an ensemble. They may also be used as a basis for studying a given work of music.

Miniature score: This is a smaller version of a full score. For this reason, it cannot be used by a conductor. However, it is still a handy tool for those looking to study a piece of music.

Study score: Study scores are sometimes similar in size and can be difficult to distinguish from miniature scores. However, study scores may include comments about the music for study purposes.

Piano score: This is a piece of sheet music that has been simplified or compressed such that it can fit on the grand staff and is therefore playable by piano. Reducing a score into a piano score takes considerable skill, since the score needs to be detailed enough to present all the elements of the composition while still remaining playable on the piano.

Vocal score: This is a full score that has been reduced to only show the vocal parts on their staves. Vocal scores make it easy and convenient for vocal performers to learn and rehearse music separately.

While these are the main types of scores, there are other minor types of scores, such as:

Short scores: These refer to scores that take a piece of music meant for many instruments and compress it to just a few staves. Short scores are typically used when composing music, then get expanded later to complete the orchestration.

Open score: This is a piece that places each voice on its own staff.

Chapter Four: Seven Step-by-Step Exercises to Help You Learn How to Read Sheet Music

Having learnt the basics of music theory, the fundamentals of music notation and the elements of sheet music, now is the time to put your knowledge into practice. Like with learning any other language, learning how to read sheet music needs lots of practice. Below is a list of step by step exercises that will speed up your learning process

Step One: Practice Full Concentration

While this may seem very obvious, it has a huge impact on your success in reading sheet music. However, without full concentration, you will easily miss notes, fly over accidentals, mess up rhythms and make a ton of other mistakes. If you are a beginner, this can be very frustrating and may even cause you to give up. Often, while trying to read a piece of music, you may find yourself reading with only half your concentration. The worst part is you might not even realize it. It's important that when you start practicing, you should clear your mind of any other distractions and focus wholly on the task at hand. The key to maintaining total concentration is to challenge yourself to complete reading an entire piece of sheet music perfectly. Try and avoid making mistakes as much as you can. If you find your mind wandering, refocus and start all over again.

Step Two: Start with Elementary Material

When starting to learn how to read sheet music, some students are often too ambitious and choose to start by reading complex musical pieces. This is not a very good approach. When learning a new language, a student starts by reading short material with simple phrases they can understand easily. As their expertise in the language grow, they graduate to reading more complex literature in the language. Similarly, you cannot learn by reading complex pieces of music. Starting with short, simple compositions allows you to acquire habits of fluency. As you get better, gradually step up the difficulty and complexity of you read. The best way to do this is to consult a qualified music teacher who can continually assess your level of knowledge and recommend suitable material.

Step Three: Divide the Music Into Chunks

During their first attempts at reading sheet music, many students try to read the music singularly. They count every single beat and take note of every single rhythm. Doing this can be very exhausting and is outright impossible. Your brain is hardwired to divide things into groups for easier comprehension. For instance, as you read this book, you are not focusing on every single letter.

Instead, your brain groups letters into words and reads them as a whole. You should do the same when it comes to reading sheet music.

A good way of practicing how to read music in chunks is to divide each bar into two parts and take note of where the downbeats fall. This allows you to interpret music in a more relaxed manner and free up your mind to focus on other aspects of the piece you are reading. This also allows you to learn how to "hear" a melody by just looking at it.

Step Four: Look for Familiar Rhythms and Patterns

Each piece of music is unique different from another. However, there are certain repeated patterns that are common in many pieces of music. Some common scale fragments are found in many musical scores. These are a great start for learning how to recognize patterns in larger music sections. Try and identify different melodic lines in the music that contain ascending or descending scale fragments. Just like children have to read multiple books to get improve their word reading skills, you should also read multiple pieces of music and strive to identify the common patterns in each. You can find practice pieces online or ask a music teacher to provide you with some.

Step Five: Practice Looking Ahead

One of the main reasons that students make mistakes when reading sheet music is the simple fact that they are not ready for the upcoming notes and are hence caught off guard. A student encounters a measure that they are supposed to play immediately and they are unable to process all this information quickly. This causes them to falter as they have to think of what is required of them at that point. Such a pause ruins the flow of the whole piece of music. To avoid being caught off guard, students should get into the practice of continuously scanning ahead to be aware of the notes and rhythms coming up. Always scan a beat or two ahead of whatever you are currently playing. This skill requires you to use a combination of all the other skills mentioned above. You have to focus fully on reading the music, divide the music into chunks and look for familiar patterns. All these allow you to be aware of whatever is coming up ahead.

Step Six: Learn to Continue Through Mistakes

As you learn how to read sheet music, it is inevitable that you are going to make some mistakes here and there. While you should aim for perfection, you should accept that you are going to make some mistakes. However, you should not let mistakes deter you. The most important thing is to always keep the tempo of the piece in mind, since this is what holds the whole music together. You might miss a note or an accidental, but just keep going and get the flow of the whole piece. Once you are done, restart the whole piece and try to eliminate the mistakes this time round.

Step Seven: Keep a Practice Journal

Like I noted earlier, the secret to becoming good at reading sheet music is practice. You should practice as many times as you can. This helps you to increase your skills and helps you build confidence in your skills. Ideally, you should practice reading sheet music at least 20 – 30 minutes each day. Each day, note down how long you spent practicing and what you practiced. Apart from practicing on your own, try to get together will friends or colleagues and practice together. This will help you improve your skills and increase your motivation.

Conclusion

The ability to read sheet music is a great skill to have. While learning how to read sheet music is a somewhat challenging task, it is something that one can teach themselves. All it requires is concentration, attention to details and lots of practice. I can't emphasize this enough. Practice is what will make you a skilled sheet music reader. As you get better, you will adopt to your own ways of reading music. This book has provided you with the fundamentals of music theory and music notation. It has also given you a basic introduction to sheet music and seven step by step exercises you can use to improve your sheet reading skills.

HOW TO PLAY
CHORDS
IN 1 DAY
The Only 7 Exercises You
Need to Learn Guitar Chords, Piano
Chords and Ukulele Chords Today
PRESTON HOFFMAN

BOOK 4

HOW TO PLAY CHORDS: IN 1 DAY

The Only 7 Exercises You Need to Learn Guitar Chords, Piano Chords and Ukulele Chords Today

Preston Hoffman

Table of Contents

Chapter One: Know Your Instruments....................................219

Chapter Two: What are Chords? 239

Chapter Three: The Seven Exercises....................................265

Chapter Four: Tips for Practicing....................................282

Chapter Five: Moving Beyond the Basics 288

Chapter Six: Chord Songs....................................292

Chapter One: Know Your Instruments

Welcome to your handy-dandy guide to learning how to play chords on the guitar, ukulele, and piano! It may come as a surprise—or it may not—to learn that all three of these instruments are quite easy to learn and you can quickly play thousands of songs on them just by following a few simple exercises and learning about the basic chords. But first, we need to break down the differences between these three instruments, since playing them will be slightly different for the chords and for your hands.

The Guitar

The guitar is the world's most popular instrument, and for good reason. It's versatile, easily portable, works well with other instruments, and is easy to learn—as you're about to find out. It has a wide range and is great for people who also enjoy singing, since you can easily play the guitar while you sing and it accompanies voices well.

There are many different types of guitars, the two main categories being acoustic and electric. It's recommended that you start with an acoustic guitar.

This here is an acoustic guitar:

And this is an electric guitar:

But there are variations within that, as well, like nylon versus steel strings, for example. Nylon strings are more mellow and easier on your fingers, while steel strings produce a bright tone and are louder. They're also harder on your fingers.

These here are nylon strings:

And these here are steel strings:

If those two images don't look too different to you, it's because the nylon is wrapped in either bronze-plated copper or in silver wire. If you're just looking at strings on a guitar, you might not be able to tell the difference at first. But you'll feel the difference in your fingers when you play them.

The best type of guitar for a beginner is a steel-strung guitar with round holes in the sideboards. They're the best for playing most of the songs you'll come across, including all of the songs in this book, and they create a good sound for accompanying singers and other instruments.

Another type of guitar is the Jumbo Guitar. It has an extra-large body, which means that it produces a better bass sound. If you're a bass player in a band, this might be the type of guitar you'd go for. This is a great guitar but with twelve strings and a larger body, it's not good for beginners:

224

It can be hard to see in this image, but where on a regular acoustic guitar like the one above each of the notches only has one string, these have two. Definitely not easy on your hands and the added musical value won't be of use to you until much later when you're further down the line in your understanding of music and can start to play around with the melodies of your songs instead of just focusing on the chords, which is what we're doing in this book.

Flamenco and Classical Guitars are strung with nylon and are used specifically for flamenco and classical music, respectively. They're good guitars and easy to learn on as a beginner but since they're for specialized music, you won't want to use them unless you're planning on playing mainly classical music.

There might not seem to be much of a difference in these guitars when you look at them, but it's all in the tuning. Flamenco guitars are designed to have a higher note register and the strings are therefore slightly different to accommodate this. Regular acoustic guitars have a lower register.

A classical guitar, on the other hand, will have a wider fret board, which can make it difficult for newer players to reach all of the strings, and they don't always have fret markers to help you out. Classical guitars just aren't designed for modern-day pop songs. Trying to play a Beatles song, for example, or that guitar classic "Wonderwall" on a classic guitar would just make it sound weird. So for our purposes, unless you want to play more classical music or more folk-sounding music, stick to regular acoustic.

Note: "Wonderwall" is considered one of the most overplayed songs on guitar, so it's best to avoid playing it.

Finally, electric guitars are the kind of guitars that can only be played when you plug them into an amplifier. You can attach pedals and other instruments to help play around with the sound of them. They're great for jazz and rock, but they might not be a good bet for a beginner. If you know your way around a guitar and want to start picking up some fancy tricks, new ways to play with sound, or you're joining a band and want to be able to be heard, then you can get an electric guitar.

Be sure to take good care of your guitar! Buy a sturdy case for it and store it in there. Hang onto the receipt after you buy it in case you're traveling with it and need to show the receipt to customs. Never let your guitar lie in the grass or dirt and be careful with it around moisture.

The Ukulele

There are, as you can tell just by looking at them, a lot of similarities between a ukulele and a guitar. However, there are also some differences to keep in mind.

First, there are the four types of ukulele: soprano, alto, tenor, and baritone—yes, just like singing voices. The soprano is the smallest, and the easiest to start out with as a beginner, since it has only four strings. The baritone is the largest and most expensive, and personally, if you're looking at a baritone then at that point you might just want to get a guitar instead.

Here is a soprano ukulele:

Here is an alto ukulele:

This is a tenor ukulele:

And finally, a baritone ukulele:

The ukulele will always sound a bit higher than the guitar, so it's natural when you're learning a song on the ukulele versus guitar for it to sound a bit higher—but the notes should still sound *right*. You'll find that it's easy for your ear to pick up the difference between notes played correctly at a higher pitch and notes that are played incorrectly. Fortunately, it's actually simpler to play chords on a ukulele than a guitar, so now that we've got you on the guitar, you'll find the transition to ukulele is pretty easy.

The most notable difference in a ukulele versus a guitar will be the strings. The tuning for a ukulele is usually GCEA:

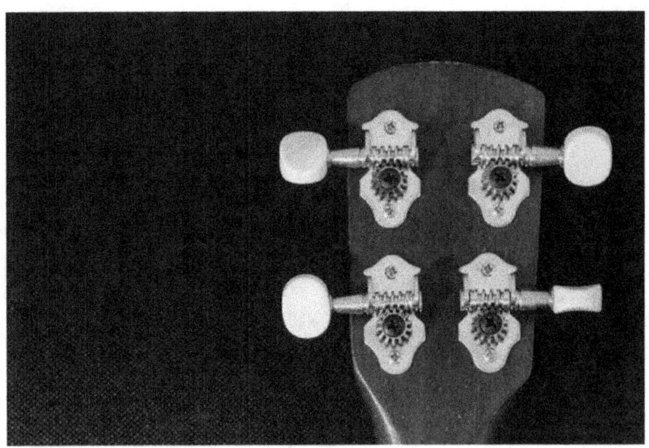

To compare this to a guitar, put a capo on the 5th fret of a guitar. A "capo" is a bar that you can buy that will hold down all of the strings on a particular fret for you. This will come in handy when you've progressed further and are performing songs where you're doing chords but can't have a finger free to hold down all the strings. With the capo on the 5th fret, play the four highest strings on your guitar. That's what it's like to play a ukulele, except that the G string on the ukulele is an octave higher even than that.

Baritone ukuleles, however, are exactly the same as the four highest strings on the guitar, no capo needed. This is why it's probably best not to buy a baritone ukulele—any song that you'd play on there you can just play on the guitar by ignoring the two lowest strings.

The Piano

The piano is probably the best known, and most beloved, of all musical instruments. Many composers started composing their pieces on piano to start with, before adding in the other instruments, and it's a versatile instrument that can handle pretty much any song that you throw at it.

A piano is, technically, a string instrument. When you press down on a key, you're actually starting up a mechanism that causes the string or strings to be plucked, causing the sound. It's also one of the most complicated instruments in the world, with 2,500 parts, and it's easily broken. The many parts of a piano include the soundboard, ribs, bridges, keys, pedals, hammers, the strings, and the cast iron plate.

Yes, a cast iron plate. It's put in over the soundboard of the piano and anchors the strings and keeps them tense so that they will vibrate properly when plucked by the hammer, which is caused by pressing on a key. The largest kind of piano is the grand piano:

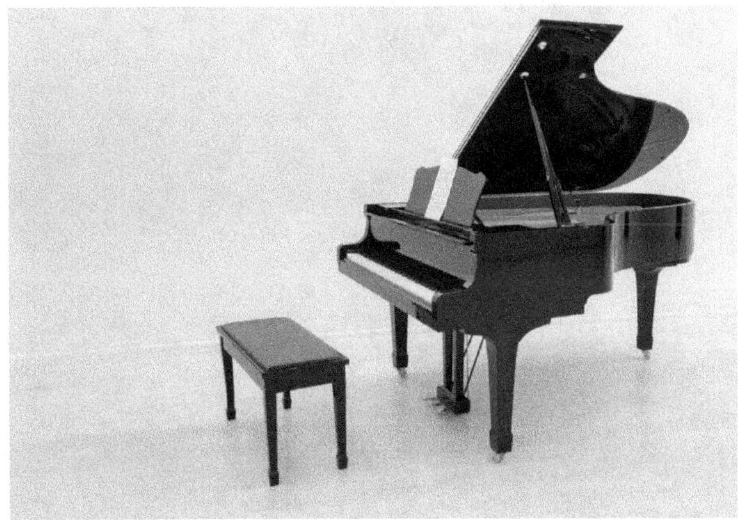

These are also known as winged pianos and are the largest in size. You would need a rather large home to fit one of these.

The next smallest is the baby grand piano, structured in every way like a grand piano, only with smaller dimensions:

The other kind of piano, and the one that most people can afford both economically and size-wise, is an upright piano:

And finally, we have the electric keyboard, the least expensive and most convenient for when you're living in a small house:

Unless you're living in an area where you have access to a grand or a baby grand, you don't need to worry about practicing on one. Practicing on a keyboard or upright piano will give you the same kind of understanding and practice, and if you're looking to perform, those are the two kinds of pianos that you'll most likely be performing on when the time comes.

Now that you understand your instruments, it's time to learn how to play them!

Chapter Two: What are Chords?

Chords are the basis for an entire song or piece of music. Without chords, you don't have a song, which is why if you know the chords of a song, you can play those same four or so notes over and over again in the rhythm of the song without learning the rest, and the audience will still recognize said song. By learning the chords through the exercises this book will teach, you'll be able to play thousands of songs. But what exactly are chords and how do they work?

What Is a Chord?

A chord is a combination of three or more notes. They're built off of a single note, known as the 'root note.' The root note will always be the first note in the chord sequence. So if you see the chord sequence C-E-G, that's a C chord. Those three notes together create a harmonious, blended sound, called the chord. When you're playing chords, whether it's guitar or piano or ukulele, you create the song by keeping your fingers in the same position, just moving them slightly up or down—so you're always playing the same notes, just as a higher or lower pitch.

How to Read Guitar and Ukulele Chords

Reading guitar and ukulele music is a bit different than reading piano music. Piano tends to use sheet music—which is important to know as a guitarist, because you'll have to read sheet music a lot of the time. Sheet music is the foundation on which all music is written, even if that music is later translated into another form, like guitar tabs.

Guitar tabs function for guitar and ukulele the way sheet music does for a piano. In fact, you can read the tabs without actually having to learn sheet music. This is part of why it's so easy to learn guitar and ukulele (and you can transfer this knowledge to the piano, as we'll discuss shortly).

Tabs are, essentially, a visual representation of where the notes are on the guitar or ukulele that you should be playing:

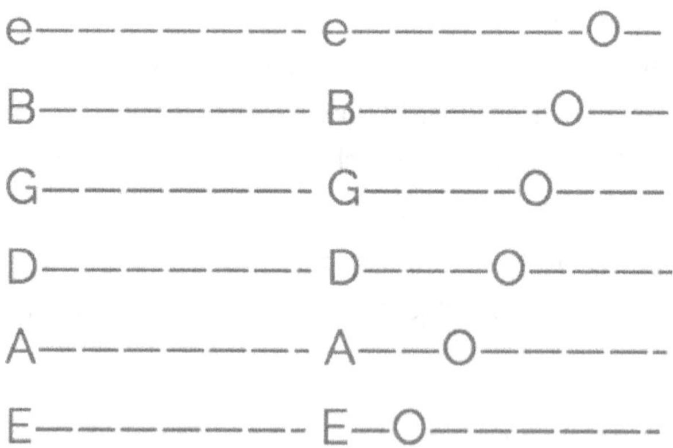

The strings on the guitar (if this was a ukulele, there would only be four strings) have the thickest, the E string, at the bottom, and the thinnest, the e string, at the top. If there is a number next to the letter, say, a 5 next to the D, that means you're placing your finger on the 5th fret of the D string. If there's a zero, that means the string is being played 'open' with no frets pressed down.

Look at that graphic again. A helpful way to remember the notes is to make an acronym for them. The one I learned was Every August Dogs Go Biting Elvis. E-A-D-G-B-E.

This is another diagram of how guitar chords might be written. The three black dots on the diagram show you which strings to press down—in this case, strings D, G, and B—and you will press down on them on the second fret. The E and A strings we're going to play open, without any frets pressed down, and the High E, or e, we're not going to play at all.

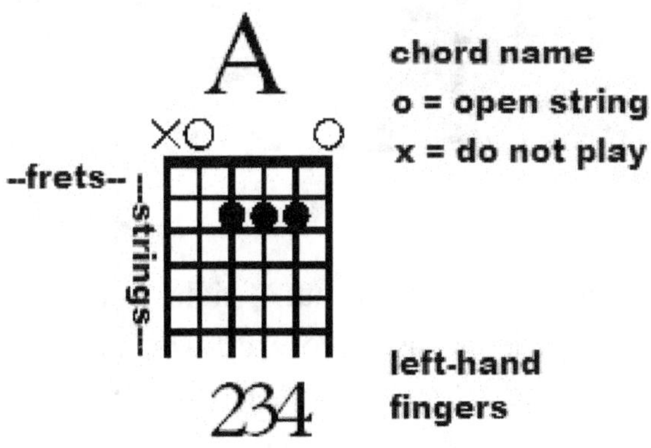

The numbers at the bottom of this chart are telling you which fingers to use to hold down the strings. Your index finger is number one, and your pinkie is number four. So for this, you'll use your middle, ring, and pinkie finger, and leave your index finger free. Keep in mind that your thumb doesn't come into play with the guitar. You use your thumb to brace against the back of the guitar so that it holds still while you move your other fingers. Here's an example of proper finger positioning:

Notice how the thumb is out of sight, bracing on the back of the guitar. The wrist is pushed forward which makes for an angle that will take some getting used to. The fingers, as you can see, are in position, so your index finger (number one) is stretching up to hit the top string.

Let's go back to that chart. So you'd put your middle finger, the 2 finger, on the D string, your ring finger, or 3 finger, on the

G string, and your pinkie or 4 finger on the B string, all on the second fret. Use the tips of your fingers only! Otherwise you'll press down on other strings and the sound will come out muffled. Then strum with your other hand. Ta-da! You're now able to read a ukulele or guitar chart and figure out what to play.

The only difference in reading between a ukulele and a guitar is that there are only four strings on a ukulele, so there's just two fewer strings to worry about. But the finger positioning and how you read the chart is all the same.

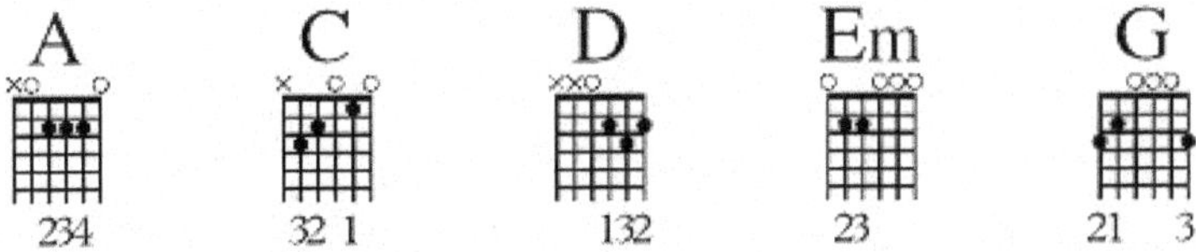

Take a look at these. We have the first one, the A chord, and now the C, D, Em, and G chords. Take a moment and figure out where your fingers go to practice reading it.

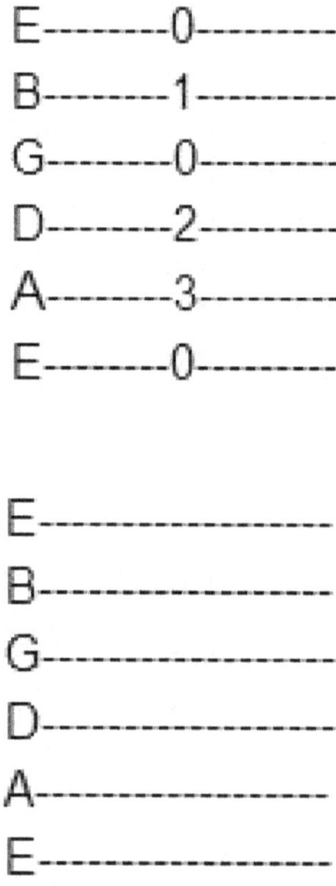

Now, look at the tabs again. The one on the right has no numbering. The one on the left has the numbering showing the fret you want to put your finger on. Unlike the previous chart, it doesn't tell you which finger—so we go with the basic principle of highest string goes to the index finger, second highest to the middle finger, and so on. For this one, you'd have your middle finger on the first fret of the B string, your ring finger on the second fret of the D string, and your pinkie on the third fret of the A string.

It's important to know these tabs because they'll help you for reading sheet music, and moving your chord exercises from guitar to the piano.

Piano Versus Guitar Chords

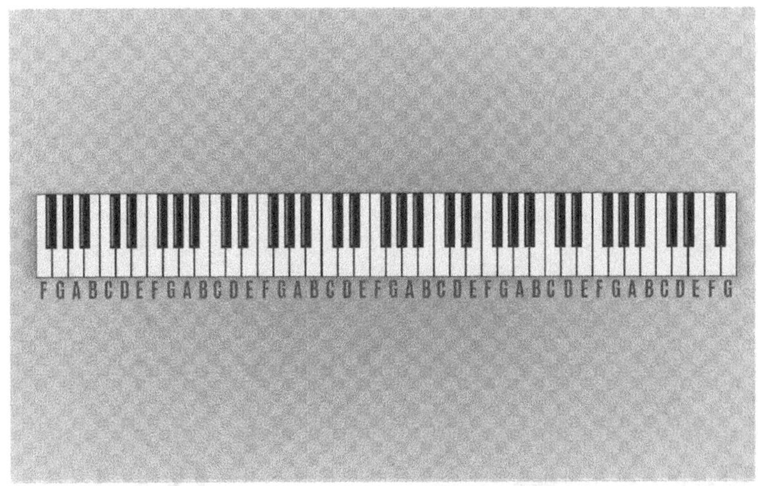

Ah, pianos. You've got a lot more room to work with than guitars, which is both a blessing and a curse when you're a beginner. Take a look at the image up above. Right away you'll notice that it has all of the notes laid out for you. Unlike a guitar, where you create the higher and lower notes by pressing down on the frets, the piano does that for you already. This means that you can play more complicated songs on the piano but it also means your fingers are going to be exhausted.

The key with playing the piano is to stretch your fingers and to keep your wrist light. This is very different from a guitar. In a guitar, if I were to grab your wrist and tug, your wrist shouldn't move. It should be firm to support the guitar neck and your fingers. A piano is the opposite—your wrist should be completely loose and relaxed to allow your fingers the most freedom of movement. If I were to press down on your wrist while you were playing piano, it should collapse.

Keep in mind as well that with both guitar and piano, each finger must move simultaneously. You will be fighting against instinct here. We have trained ourselves to treat our fingers as one unit, to pick things up, to throw things, and so on. Typing is arguably the only thing where our fingers move independently of one another. But look at this picture below:

Note how the thumb is down on the keyboard but the other fingers are not. The thumb is moving independently of the others. If you move one finger on a piano or guitar, the other fingers shouldn't move at all.

Take a look at this picture:

Notice how the hands seem to dip down a little from the wrist, and the fingers are slightly curled. Like with guitar, you want your fingertips to be the ones making the notes, not your whole hand. See how relaxed the wrist is to allow the hand to droop like that? With the guitar, it's all about wrist strength. With piano, it's about wrist relaxation. But with both, remember, you need fingertips and finger flexibility.

Now, like guitar, a piano chord is any set of three or more notes played simultaneously. Note the image below:

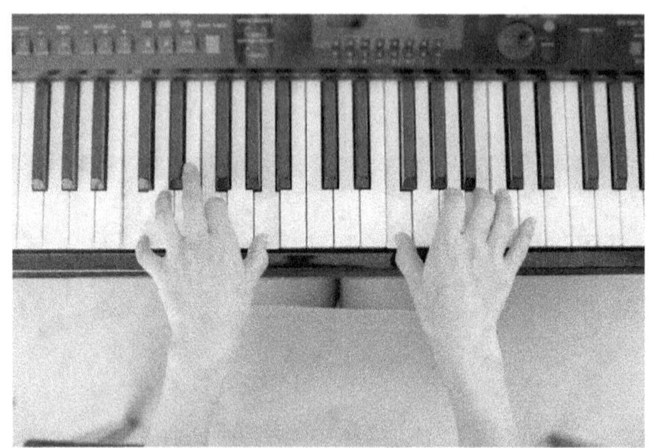

The person's fingers are pressing down on keys while there is are white keys in between them. The thumb, middle finger, and pinkie of the person's right hand are pressing down on the white keys. This creates a chord the same way you do on a guitar. Most piano chords, and certainly these basic ones, will be made with your thumb, middle finger, and pinkie.

The person's left hand is doing the same thing—here is where you can get in some variation. In a guitar, for example, when you're playing the four or five notes with just your one hand, using all of your fingers. As you can see from the image above, those same four or five notes are played with both of your hands. Pressing down on the notes with both hands will create the chord for a piano, while strumming with one hand while the other holds down the strings creates the chord for a guitar or ukulele.

Now, fingers are numbered when you play piano, just like with the guitar. The only difference is that the thumb is included with piano, so instead of the index finger being number one, the thumb is number one, and you go on with the pinkie being number five. So most chords are 1-3-5 chords, using your thumb, middle finger, and pinkie, on three alternating notes.

Alternating is something you're going to come up against in both piano and guitar/ukulele. Now, there are half-steps and full-steps in notes. In a piano, a half-step is when you go from a white key to a black key, or vice versa. You're going from one note to the one directly above or below it. So if you're on the white key C, then go up to the nearest black key, C#, that's a half step. A full-step is where you go up two notes, or one 'full note.' You're not going up from a C to a C sharp or down to a C flat. It's just a full note, so from C to D—which is the next white key.

The only exception? When you're going from white key E. The F key is the same thing as an E#.

All you need to worry about, though, is that when making your chords go from guitar to piano, you put your thumb, or 1 finger, on the root note. Let's say it's C. You would then count up two full-steps. So you'd count up: C#, then D, then D#, then E. So you put your middle finger on E. Then count up two more full-steps: E, F/E#, then F#, to put your pinkie on G.

Now you have the C chord, C-E-G. This is called a major chord, by the way. A minor chord is the opposite. You would put your thumb on C, then go up only one full-step and one half-step, so you wouldn't go all the way up to E—you'd stop at D#. Then you'd put your pinkie on the same place, G. An easy way to remember this? Just put your fingers in position for the chord, then move your middle finger up one half-step.

This is an easy way to have fun with songs, by the way. Play any chord song, but move your middle finger up so that it's now in minor key. It'll sound cool and unusual and completely change how the song sounds.

Another way to help with figuring out the differences in your hands on the piano versus your one hand on the guitar is to imagine the three lowest guitar strings as what you play with your left hand on the piano, and the three highest strings as what you play with your right hand. So let's say you've got your five fingers on five strings on the guitar. Your left hand would take some of those notes, while your right hand would take the others, on the piano. You're just dividing up the notes in a different way, but you still play them all at the same time. A good rule of thumb is that your left hand on the piano plays the root note (so C, for C-E-G), and your right hand plays the others.

But what about sheet music?

That right there probably looks very intimidating. Never fear, though, you won't be learning any of that here—in fact, you won't have to. If you want to play more complicated, classical pieces, then you can learn those once you've mastered these basics, but we're here to learn chords that will allow you to sit down and play the songs that come on the radio. This will, in turn, give you the basic understanding that you'll need if you want to play these more complicated pieces but in the meantime, you'll make a killing serving as the human jukebox for your friends. So, sheet music!

This is a piece of blank sheet music. The first thing you should notice should already be familiar to you—the lines are just like the guitar strings on the guitar tabs we just learned. These lines are called the staff or staves, by the way. This is where you'll see the notes, rather like where you'll see the notations on the tab for which fret to hold down. However, unlike the tabs, which just tell you which fret, notes will tell you how long to hold the note for, so you can look at the sheet music and learn the rhythm even if you don't previously know the song.

This symbol here on the left is called a clef. This indicates the pitch of the notes that you're playing. F, C, and G are the usual types of clef. This here is a G clef, the one you'll probably recognize the most easily.

This here is an F clef.

And this:

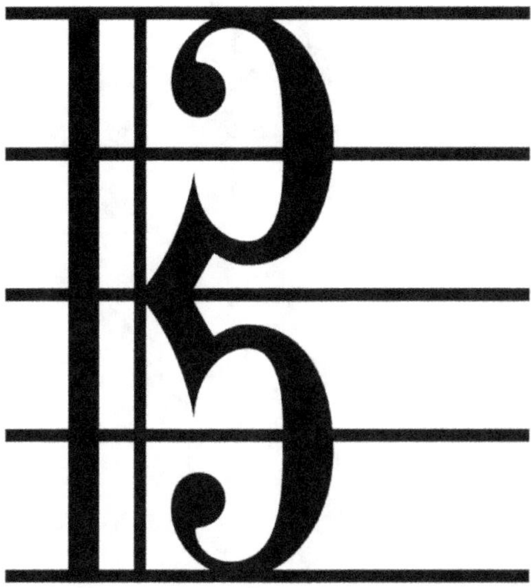

Is a C clef. The G clef is the one that you'll come across the most often. You probably haven't even seen a C clef before. As you noticed in the image of the blank sheet music, there's a G and an F clef. A G clef is also known as a treble clef, and indicates higher notes, which is why it's higher on the lines. The F clef is also known as a bass clef and means lower notes. You won't often have to deal with such lower notes on your chords, not unless you choose to make your song lower in pitch.

But what are those symbols next to that image of the G clef? Those are 'key signatures.' They indicate how many sharps and flats are in a piece. You won't often need these but they can be helpful when you're going to play a chord to remember this when you're trying to remember which note is which that you're playing.

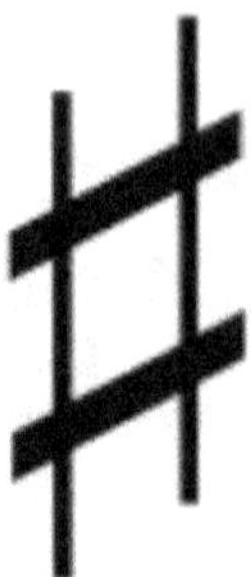

This symbol here is a sharp.

And this symbol is a flat.

Note that you'll run into sharps more than you'll run into flats. So if you're playing and you see a letter with one of these symbols after it, it will tell you to place your finger on the white key, and then either move it up a half-step to the nearest black key (a sharp) or down a half-step to the nearest black key (a flat).

The number of sharps and flats next to a clef will tell you what key the piece of music is in. The position of the flats and sharps tells you whether it's an F sharp or a G sharp or so on, and judging by how many there are and what position they're in you'll be able to know what key signature this is in.

This is helpful to keep in the back of your mind for playing classical pieces, but again, it's not necessary for knowing how to play the chords for songs.

Go back and look at the image of the blank sheet music again. You'll see that it ends at the edge of a page. This is called a bar. It will tell you that the measure, or period of time for this part of the music, is over. The number of beats per measure can vary, but there will be however many notes on the sheet music as there are beats, and then at the end there will be the bar. So if you're trying to figure out how many notes are in a measure, count the notations, and when you've reached the bar, you know how many there are—if you counted eight, then there are eight, and so on. The more notes, the faster the piece.

Unlike a guitar or ukulele, where you have to know the song to know how the rhythm goes, the piano music will tell you.

This is a whole note. You hold it four a count of four:

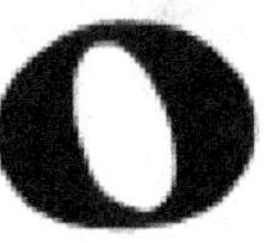

This is a half note. You hold it for a count of two:

This is an ordinary note. Technically it's a quarter note, but it's the most common note that you'll find. You hold it for a single beat:

Sometimes you'll run into these notes:

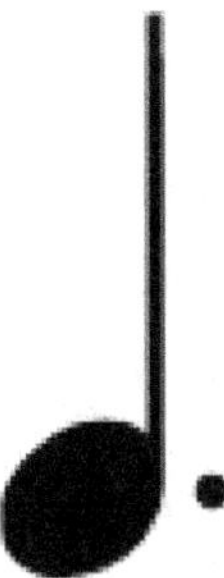

This dot serves as a half beat. Normally, you're multiplying and dividing by two—a quarter note is one beat, a half note is two beats, and a whole note is four beats. When you see a dot next to this, it means add half of the note's value. So this dot is next to a quarter note, meaning you add half a beat. If it were next to a half note, you'd add one beat, making the entire note three beats long.

This is an eighth note:

As you can imagine, eighth notes are very short, half a beat. They are always half a beat, unlike dots, which can change in value based on the note they're next to. A dot is half the value of the note it's next to, so the value of the dot changes depending on whether it's accompanying a quarter or whole or half note. An eighth note is always half a beat, no matter what other note it's with.

If you ever see a symbol like this:

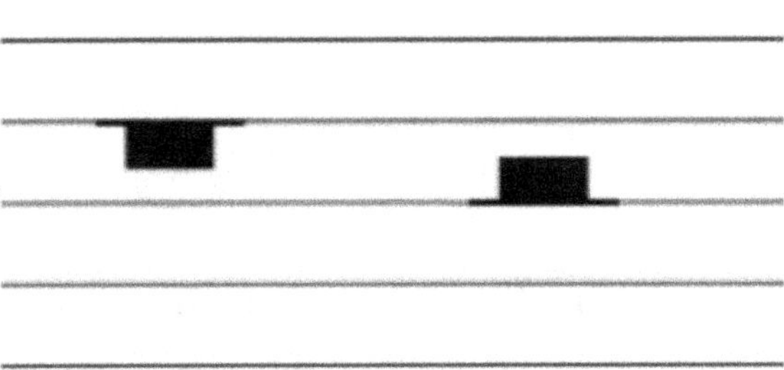

Whether it's facing up or down, that means it's a rest.
Facing down, it's a whole rest, so four beats. Facing up, it's a half
rest, or two beats.

These indicate shorter rests:

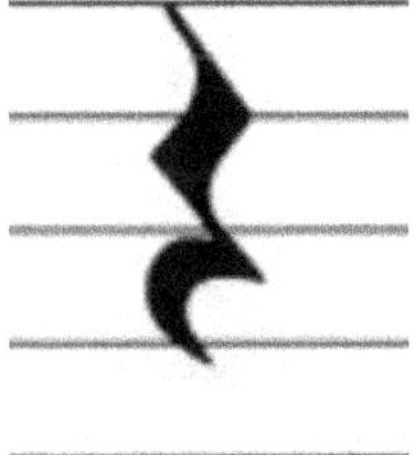

This is a quarter rest.

And this is an eighth rest. You count them just like you count the musical notes, but you don't play anything. These symbols stand for silence, and once again they indicate to you the rhythm of a piece.

Learning these basics of piano sheet music are helpful because while you can learn a song using guitar tabs for the guitar and ukulele, if you're ever unsure about the rhythm of a piece, you can look it up on sheet music and see how long each note is and figure out the rhthym.

Vocabulary

Here are some terms that you'll need to be familiar with, especially for piano, for when you pick up sheet music or if you are performing with others.

- Playing in Different Keys: This means that the position of your finger stays the same but the root note changes. For example, "I'm playing in F major instead of C major." Same chord position, but different notes, because you moved your fingers higher or lower on the guitar or piano.

- Arrangement: This is for if you're playing with a group. The arrangement decides who is playing what notes on the chord, which tempos, and when.
- Chord Extensions: This means adding alterations to a chord, which can make it sound completely different even if the basic notes are the same.
- Rhythm: This is how many pop songs can sound different even though they are all using the same chord. The rhythm is one of the first things that people notice when listening to a song, so changing it up can change the song almost completely.
- Melody: These are the varying notes that you play over the base chord—again, a way to take the same chord and make it sound different.
- Lyrics: You probably know this one already, but lyrics are the words that someone sings in time to the music.
- Adagio: This means to go slowly.
- Allegro: This means to play quickly.
- Beat: This is another word for rhythm.
- Leggiero: This is used mostly in piano, and means to play 'lightly' without putting too much force on the keys.
- Time Signature: How many beats are in each bar of music. So if there are eight beats, then the time signature is eight. The more beats, the faster you play.

- Bridge: A transitional passage. The repeated lyrics that a singer sings just before the chorus is the bridge—it literally 'bridges' the versus to the chorus.
- Chorus: The repeated phrase of the song, the heart of the song's meaning and music.
- Measure: One complete cycle of the time signature.
- Meter: This is the pattern of the rhythm. Think of it as the pauses in between the beats.
- Forte: To play strong and powerfully.
- Piano: This isn't the instrument—if someone says to play piano, it means to play it gently.
- Tempo: This is the overall speed of the piece. The meter and beat and rhythm make up the tempo.
- Rest Signs: This indicates when you stop playing your instrument and let it 'rest' for a period of time. This is usually done when you're playing with other instruments, so you all get your turn in the spotlight.
- Notes: The indication of what string or key you should be playing and for how long. Depending on the shape or shading of the note, it'll tell you how long to hold it for.

Chapter Three: The Seven Exercises

Now that you understand what your instruments are, how they work, how to read and understand music and bar chords, you're fully equipped to sally forth and play these instruments like a pro. Here are the seven basic exercises that will help you to play pretty much any song in the world.

Exercise One:

We're going to start with a C Major chord. This is the easiest chord to learn. Lots of songs, including "Are We Out of the Woods" by Taylor Swift and "Stay with Me" by Sam Smith use this key.

So, if you're on a guitar or ukulele, put your index finger on the first fret of the second string (B string). Then put your middle finger on the fourth string, on the second fret (this is the D string). Your ring finger goes on the third fret of the fifth string, or A string, and that's it! You don't play the sixth string, E, and the other two strings, e and G, are played open, so no fingers on those frets. Here's a picture of what that looks like on a guitar:

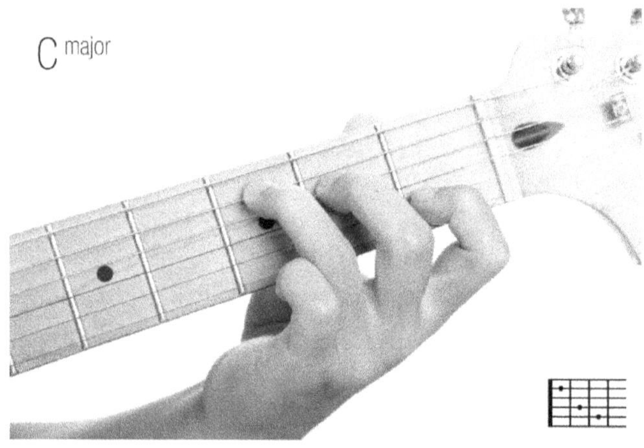

To play this on piano, you want to do these three keys that are in red:

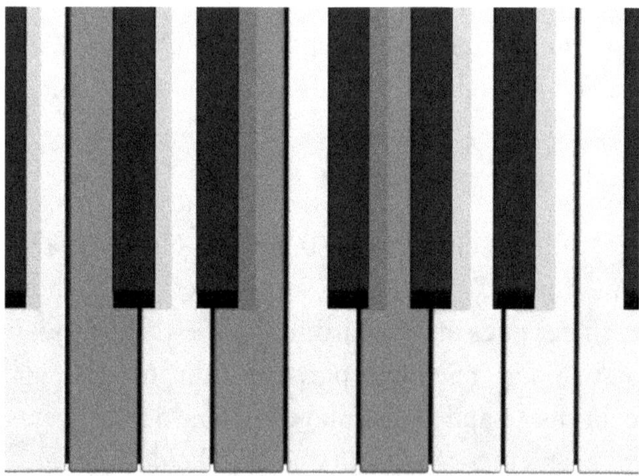

You can play them in any part of the piano, it's still the same chord. Practice doing it on the piano and on the guitar—

remember to only strum five of the strings, not the E string—and on the ukulele, until you can do it in a steady rhythm of one, two, three, four.

To get an idea of how rhythm can completely change this song, do this chord while singing "Are We Out of the Woods" by Taylor Swift. You can play the song itself to accompany you if you feel more comfortable with that. Feel how fast that chord is. Then play "Stay with Me" by Sam Smith. This is very slow, with the chord playing, and then a long rest. That change in rhythm completely changes how the song feels.

Exercise Two:

Next exercise is the G major chord! "You Shook Me All Night Long" by AC/DC and "Heart of Gold" by Birdy are two G major chord songs, and again, very different in sound because of the rhythm.

Put your index finger on second fret of the fifth string, or A string. Then put your middle finger on the third fret of the bottom string, the E string. Your ring finger goes on the third fret of the e string, the first string, and your pinkie doesn't have to do anything. Keep in mind that your index and middle fingers have to be arched up so they don't accidentally brush other strings. This is where using your fingertips is important.

Here's an image of what your hand should look like:

Here is that same chord on the piano:

The red are the ones you want to be hitting. Use your
fingertips on your thumb, middle finger, and pinkie, so that you
don't hit any other keys while you're playing this. Again, practice
just doing this on your guitar and piano and ukulele as just a one,

two, three, four beat rhythm. Don't try to rush things. Try out the two songs, by Birdy and AC/DC, just to feel the difference the rhythm and the melody of the singer can do to change a song that has the same chords.

Exercise Three:

Next we're doing the D chord. This is an important chord on guitar for pop songs, so while you wouldn't normally learn it as quickly if you were studying piano for classical music, you're going to learn it here so that you can play all those songs on piano and guitar easily. Songs that use the D Major Chord include "Send My Love (to Your New Lover)" by Adele and "The Boys are Back in Town" by Thin Lizzy.

Put your index finger on the second fret of the fourth string, or G string. Then put your middle finger on the second fret of the sixth string, the e string, and then put your ring finger on the third fret of the fifth or B string.

If this chord seems a little more difficult for your fingers to handle on the guitar, that's how it should be. Some other very common chords that we're going to learn next are going to have four notes in them instead of just three, so this D major chord will help you, especially so that you can learn the F Major chord for the next exercise.

This is what this chord looks like on the guitar:

And this is what it looks like on piano:

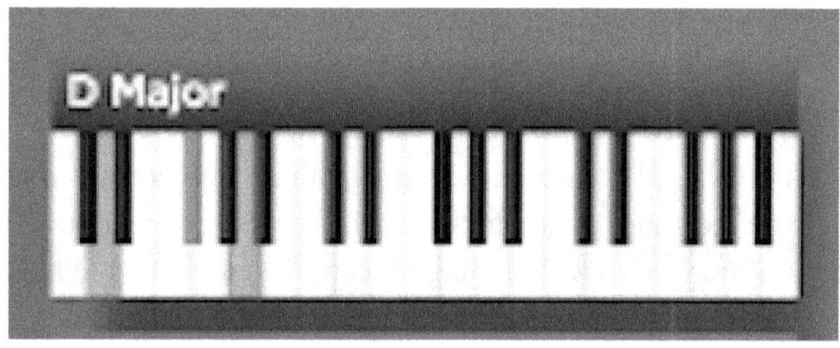

Notice that for this you're using one black key on the piano. Practice strumming on guitar or ukulele and getting the rhythm on the piano, using the two songs as accompaniment to help you if you feel you need it. Having a song in mind as your goal can be helpful as it helps you to integrate the idea of a rhythm into your playing.

Exercise Four:

Now we're getting into that F Major Chord that we mentioned. "Still Into You" by Paramore, "What's My Age Again?" by Blink-182, and "Ain't No Rest for the Wicked" by Cage the Elephant are all in this key. It's a popular one.

This is the first chord that uses four fingers on the guitar, and it's difficult because it's a bar chord. This means you have to take your index finger and put it down across the first fret on all of the strings. Yup, all of them. This will take some getting used to because your finger needs to build up the strength to hold all six strings (or four strings, for the ukulele) down at the same time.

Keep in mind that your finger shouldn't be directly on the fret. Rather, it should be directly behind the fret. So when you put your finger on, say, the second fret of the D string, your fingertip should actually be right before the line of the fret. This actually gives you less work to do as the fret can then do its job to hold the string in place and help it resonate. If you ever pluck a guitar string and it doesn't have a clear, resonating sound, it's probably because your finger is on the fret rather than behind it.

So, put your index finger across all the strings on the first fret. Then put your middle finger on the second fret of the third or G string, your ring finger on the third fret of the fifth or A string, and your pinkie on the third fret of the fourth or D string. This is how it should look on guitar:

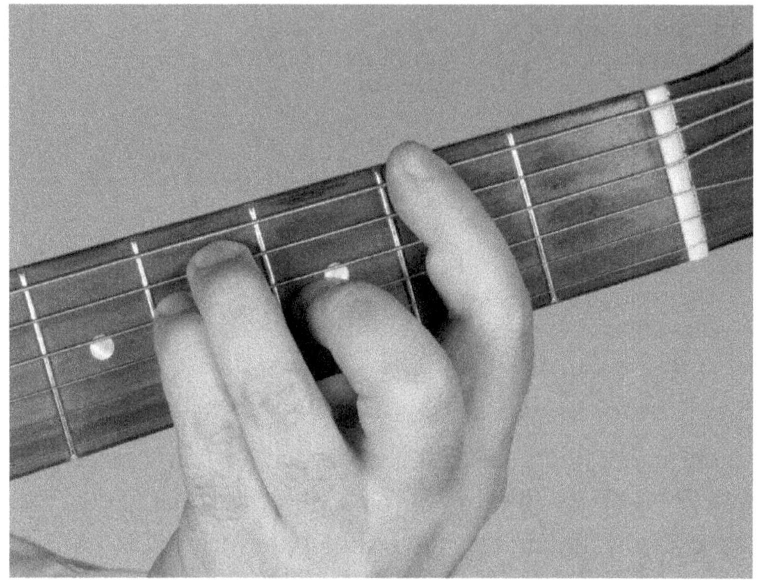

    Notice how the index finger looks curved? You're going to have to do that in order to cover all of the frets while giving your other fingers the room to press on their strings.

On piano, however, this is one of the easiest chords. It looks like this:

You don't even have to stretch your fingers. Practice with this chord as well and get the feel for it.

Exercise Five:

We're going to get really fancy now. This exercise, you're going to practice doing a chord progression.

Songs progress from one chord to another, generally in four sets. So you'll have four sets of three or four notes that you repeat, over and over again. Take the F Major Chord that we just used. You won't keep your fingers on the same fret the entire song, but you will keep them in the same position. You just slide your hand up or down to hit different notes. Same with a piano.

To play the full song, you keep your fingers in the same position and just move your and up or down the keyboard or neck of your guitar and ukulele.

For example, for "Ain't No Rest for the Wicked" by Cage the Elephant, you get your hands into the F major position. You start on the third fret. Then move your hand until the index finger is on the fifth fret. Now move it so your index finger is on the eighth fret. Now move your index finger to the first fret. Now back down to the third fret.

You've now just played the entirety of the song, all without moving your fingers, just sliding your hand up and down and strumming to the beat. Do that with all of the songs on guitar and piano and ukulele: find the notes on the sheet music and move your hands up and down until you've got it all down.

Exercise Six:

So, our next mission: practicing those chord progressions. Let's take a look at this handy dandy chart:

See how you can look at the notes both on piano sheet music, on the charts, and on guitar tabs? Chord progressions are often written in roman numerals. So G major is I, and C major is IV.

The list of progressions at the bottom is what you need to practice. You switch your fingers from chord to chord. Start just with the four that you know. The I-V-vi-IV chord progression, or

275

G-D-em-C, is one of the most common in pop music. The only difference is the rhythm and which one of these four you start on, but it's the same order. So if you start on C, the next three notes are G, D, and em, then back to C again. If you start on D, then it's em, C, and then G before back to D. If you just practice going through these four, going slowly, then you can find you're playing pretty much every pop song that you know.

What's a metronome, you ask? This handy-dandy little thing:

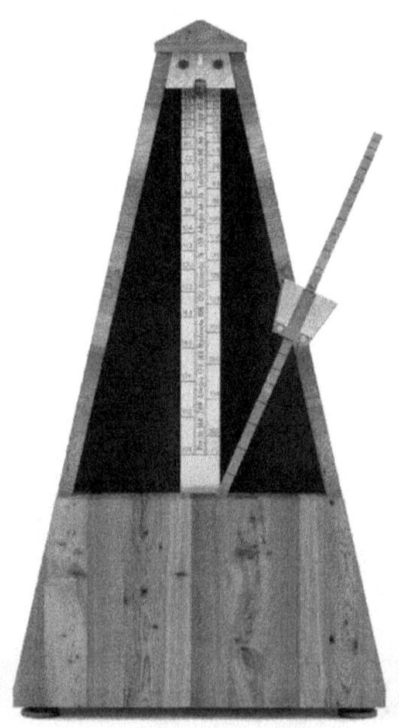

You can get a version on your phone or computer if you don't want to buy one. It keeps time for you. Put it on a slow setting and try to strum, or if you're on piano press down, in time with the metronome. This will help you improve your sense of rhythm while you do these chord progressions.

It's okay if you can't get all of these chord progressions right away. But by now your fingers will have gotten used to the positions on the piano and on the guitar, and you can always go back to the earlier exercises if you need. Just keep following these chord progressions until you're able to move back and forth smoothly between them.

Exercise Seven:

Here are some more chord progressions, this time in E major! What is E major for guitar and piano? It's a little more difficult, so here are some visuals:

You want your index finger on the fourth string on the first fret, your middle finger on the second string on the second fret, and your ring finger on the third string, also in the second fret—which is where it gets tricky, since you're having two fingers share that same space and need to press down on both strings in the same place. Your pinkie can stay out of the way. "Back in Black" by AC/DC and "Pour Some Sugar on Me" by Def Leppard are two songs in the key of E Major.

Here's what it looks like on piano:

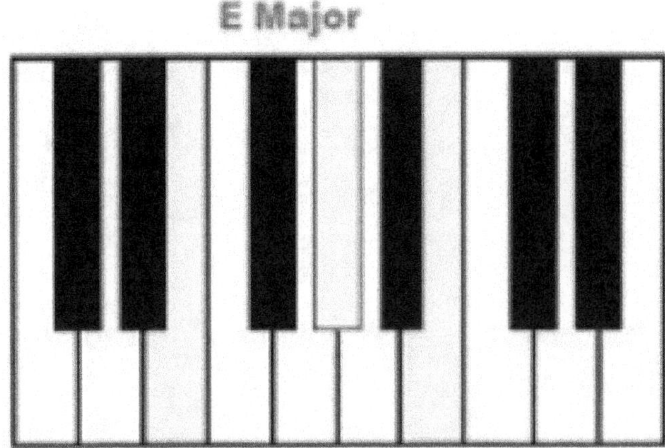

Again, much easier on piano than on guitar. You'll find that most of these chord progressions are easier to do on the piano rather than on guitar or ukulele, whereas reading sheet music for piano is harder than reading tabs and charts for guitar. It's a give and take, but both instruments are easily translatable into the other.

Here are the chord progressions for E Major:

Look at it as a chart, as a tab, as sheet music, and as roman numerals. The more you practice, the more you'll be able to just look at any one of these and understand. Go through the chord progressions on this sheet, and the previous one, and you'll know pretty much everything there is to know about playing basic songs by the time that you're through.

It's almost unbelievable how easy it is to pick all of this up—constant practice is the key, but with these fundamentals, you'll be wowing your friends and family in no time. In the next chapter, we'll explore some tips to keep in mind not just as you do these exercises but as you progress further.

Chapter Four: Tips for Practicing

So now we're going to go over some random tips that'll help you out as you're practicing. Keep in mind that everyone learns just a little bit differently, so what might work for one person won't work for you. But these are all things to keep in mind as you practice the seven exercises:

Tip #1:

Practice doing your chord shapes one finger at a time, if you're having trouble remember where to keep all of your fingers. Starting with just one finger at a time can help take the pressure off and keep you from getting confused. There's no harm in starting slow.

Tip #2:

Practice the chord shapes without strumming. Again, no harm in starting slow if that's what you need. The key here is to get those chords memorized so that you can play any song that you want, so don't rush forward if you don't have those.

Tip #3:

Pay attention to the chord changes. Transitions are the hardest thing to get down, so you'll want to practice those a lot. It'll seem hard at first, switching the positions of your fingers, more so on guitar than on piano since you're bending your wrist into an odd shape. With piano, the struggle will be teaching your fingers how to stretch out. But don't get discouraged! Practice transitions.

Tip #4:

Keep your metronome slow. I know, you want to go fast! And you'll be surprised by how fast even the slower songs feel once you start playing them. Getting these exercises down is what matters, not the speed.

Tip #5:

Make a practice plan and stick to it. This can go both ways—don't overbook yourself, but don't sell yourself short, either. Plan for a good amount of time that works easily with your schedule. Otherwise you'll find yourself making excuses. Say, for example, you've planned to practice for an hour every day. But when you get home from work, you find that the idea of practicing for a whole hour is just too draining. So you make excuses to not do it, thinking you'll make up the time later. Or, conversely, say you've promised yourself that you'll practice for ten minutes a day—and then get frustrated when you're not making a lot of progress. Find a time that isn't too ambitious but still gives you a good solid bit to practice your exercises.

Tip #6:

Find a chord dictionary so that when you've progressed beyond the more basic chords of these songs you can learn new ones and keep in practice. It's amazing the amount of chords and chord variations that are out there, and once you've mastered these, you can get really fancy and wow everyone. This is especially true of piano—once you've mastered these exercises and chords, go ahead and get a beginner's piano book with some classical pieces in it. You'll be surprised at how many you'll be able to play!

Tip #7:

It's important to keep your fingers and wrists healthy. Remember that with piano, your wrist is supposed to be completely relaxed, and your fingertips have to do a lot of stretching but remain light. With guitar and ukulele, your wrist has to be strong and in position, and your fingertips have to be strong to put the right amount of pressure on the strings. It can be easy for you to hurt your fingers and wrists over time if you don't do proper exercises. Take time to bend your wrists, rotate them, clench and unclench your fist (a small exercise ball is good for this) and practice lifting and extending your fingers and holding the position. It might seem silly, but doing these exercises before you play will help to prevent hand cramps and wrist pain later on. Below is an example of some wrist exercises that you can to do help keep your wrists flexible, strong, and healthy. A ten-minute warm up for your fingers and wrists might very well seem silly, but carpel tunnel syndrome and other health hazards have seriously affected the performance of guitarists and pianists for years, including famous ones. It's better to do some warming up than to spend months in pain and unable to practice.

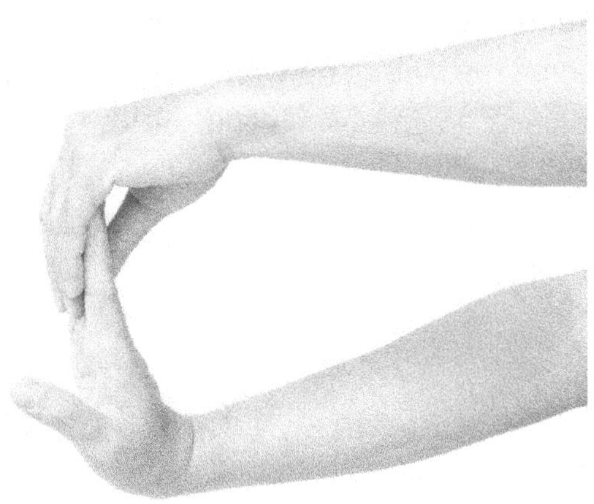

Tip #8:

If you find yourself getting frustrated or tired, or like you want to smash your piano to bits, then take a break. Walk away and get some fresh air. You won't learn if you find yourself hating practice, so go easy on yourself!

Tip #9:

Regular practice is better than how much you practice. Practicing for twenty minutes a day is better than practicing for two hours once a week. You want the repetition to get into your fingers.

Tip #10:

Count out loud as you practice your rhythms when you're doing these chords. It might sound silly, but it helps you to integrate the rhythm into your head. Some prefer, for example, to count using numbers. Others use phrases corresponding to the notes on the sheet music: "whole note hold it," for a whole note, or "quarter dot" for a quarter note with a dot on it. Whatever you use doesn't matter so long as you say it out loud to practice.

Tip #11:

Explore and have fun! Go onto the internet and find videos that show you how to play new songs. Go to a local jam session or open mike night at a café and perform for some people. Try writing your own songs or playing around with chord combinations. You learned these instruments because you wanted to, so don't lose sight of that. Do this for your own enjoyment.

Chapter Five: Moving Beyond the Basics

Ideas to keep in mind as you progress to more complicated chords, especially on the piano, and the idea of songwriting, and how these instruments can all play together at the same time.

Keep in mind chord changes and how they affect the song. You want your transitions to be smooth, for the sound to be clear and to resonate, and for you to get good at knowing where to place your fingers without having to pause and look.

Piano and guitar, and even ukulele, are great instruments for accompanying singers. You're going to get a lot of requests to accompany people when they want to sing a song, and you're probably going to want to sing a song yourself while providing your own accompaniment. As you gain confidence, you'll be tempted to really let your playing skills shine. Don't! The melody, and therefore the singer, is the star of the show. Practice playing at the right volume without too much energy so that you don't drown out the singer and steal the show, even if it's from yourself. After all, your chords are great but what if no one can hear what you're singing?

You're going to sometimes run into a problem where you have a piece on guitar tabs that you want to translate to piano sheet music, and vice versa. Doing this should wait until you've gotten comfortable with chord progressions and the exercises listed previously. You'll be able to figure out dozens of songs just by doing the chord progressions using different rhythms and accompanying a recording of a song (it can help to get an instrumental copy of said song, so the singer doesn't distract you with her melody). But when the time comes, here's a good example using the classic "Stairway to Heaven":

Tabs and sheet music are, fortunately, both on lines. So you would start by looking at what line the first note is on. It should say 7 and be on the third line from the bottom: the seventh fret of the D string. Now, you count backwards seven frets until you get to the open string—and count backwards on the piano at the same time. D, D#, E, F, F#, G, G#, and then ending on A. So the first note you'd play for this on the piano is A.

You just keep transcribing that way, counting backwards on the piano from how many frets there are on the guitar, to find each note. It's time consuming, but once you've moved past the beginning stages and want to learn more complicated songs like "Stairway to Heaven," you'll find yourself in this position a lot.

Piano can be especially difficult to learn as you progress further in your understanding of music. With the guitar, you'll want to start to simply incorporate the melody—this means plucking individual strings in between the strumming of the chords. But integrating the piano melody can take a lot of practice as you're moving both hands in different ways simultaneously. This is where fundamentals are important. Return to your chords when you feel frustrated and keep practicing those. Work on tapping each individual key out to improve your fingers' ability to move independently. And do the fundamentals like learn your scales. They're not necessary to learn for these chord songs, but if you want to move beyond that into more classical pieces, then you'll have to start learning them.

As you progress, you'll start to develop your own personal style. You might add a little flair to your version of "Don't Stop

Believing" by Journey, or perhaps you moved your middle finger up to switch to a minor key for when you play "Hey, Jude" by the Beatles on the piano. That is totally right and natural to do. Embrace your personal style and as you grow in confidence, experiment. Experimenting on already-existing chords and chord songs is how new chord songs are made, so have at it.

If you want to start getting into songwriting, there are tons of ways that you can go about it. Tom Waits, a singer-songwriter, would play multiple radios at once to find where the songs overlapped in their chords. You might find that the chords of one song would match the riff of another, and combining them makes your own song.

Another way to do it is don't give yourself time to second-guess anything. Set a timer for fifteen minutes. You now have to get your song written in that time. Ready, set, go! This eliminates your ability to second-guess yourself and agonize over a particular chord. You never know what you'll find when you're racing against the clock.

And sometimes, just stop listening to music. Stare out the window for a while. Revel in the silence. Spend a day not talking, just listening to everything around you. Shutting off one of your sensory inputs or outputs, whether it's forcing yourself to just stare out of your skylight, promising yourself not to talk, or not listening to anything. Removing one sense can heighten the others and give your brain a chance to rest and see things in a new way that might give you the inspiration that you need.

If you've moved past the chord progressions and have learned the songs in this book and still want to go further, remember, you can always get yourself a teacher. Even if that 'teacher' is someone on the internet who posts videos about their work on ukulele or piano or whatnot, they can be a source of inspiration and added learning for you as you move farther along in your study of music. There's only so much that you can learn on your own without someone helping to walk you through the more complicated parts, so if you find yourself moving past the chord songs and want to challenge yourself, a teacher can be someone to help walk you through that.

Similarly to that, join in the conversation in the music world! Look up what musicians are saying about their work, listen to new songs, join a band, go listen to an open mike night. You can't operate in a vacuum and collaborating with others, even if that collaboration is just you sitting and listening, is an important part of the artistic process. Find a group of people that you can share ideas with and who you can learn from. You'd be surprised at how it helps improve not only your playing but your understanding of music in general.

Chapter Six: Chord Songs

Here is a list of different songs that you can play using the basic chords. Most of them use the most popular "pop music" chord that we previously discussed, but others use some of the six other chords. Now that you know the basic chords you can play any of these songs with ease—you just have to learn the tempo. One of my personal favorites, and the song that I started learning when I was a beginner, is "Ain't No Rest for the Wicked" by Cage the Elephant. If you're a little amazed by how many songs are on here, just think of how your friends will feel when you sit down at a piano or whip out your guitar or ukulele and find that you've turned into a musical genius. It's all in those basic chords.

Something to keep in mind is that the melody will vary from song to song. That's not actually what matters when playing the song, though. If you play the right chord, in the right rhythm, you'll actually be fine. In fact in a lot of bands, one guitar plays just the chords while the other plays the melody. If you have the chords down, the audience will know the song—especially if you're singing, because your voice then carries the melody so you don't have to worry about actually doing it with your guitar. Helpful, right?

I-V-vi-IV Songs:

The following songs are songs that are done using the most common chord, I-V-vi-IV. Many people have pointed out the use of this chord in pop songs, and while some would argue it's overused, this is good news for you because with this chord you can play hundreds of different songs using this one chord. Songs that use this chord include:

Don't Stop Believing by Journey

You're Beautiful by James Blunt

Forever Young by Alphaville

I'm Yours by Jason Mraz

Hey Soul Sister by Train

Wherever You Will Go by The Calling

Can You Feel the Love Tonight by Elton John (from The Lion King)

Take Me Home, Country Roads by John Denver

She Will Be Loved by Maroon Five

Let it Be by The Beatles

When I Come Around by Green Day

Save Tonight by Eagle Eye Cherry

Africa by Toto

Behind These Hazel Eyes by Kelly Clarkson

One of Us by Joan Osborne

Complicated by Avril Lavigne

Apologize by OneRepublic

Otherside by Red Hot Chili Peppers

Kids by MGMT

Superman by Five for Fighting

Going by Key:

Another way that you can look up songs is to look them up by the major chord. The following are songs divided by the chords that we learned in our exercises.

C Major Songs:

Happier by Ed Sheeran

Heaven by Bryan Adams

How Does it Feel by Avril Lavigne

Sweetest Devotion by Adele

When My Heart Beats Like a Hammer by B.B. King

Bang Bang by Ariana Grande

Stay with Me by Sam Smith

Are We Out of the Woods by Taylor Swift

Minority by Green Day

Stockholm Syndrome by Muse

Use Somebody by Kings of Leon

Wanted (Dead or Alive) by Bon Jovi

Stay by Rihanna featuring Mikky Echo

G Major Songs:

Under the Tide by Chvrches

Make You Feel Better by Red Hot Chili Peppers

Wake by Linkin Park

You Shook Me All Night Long by AC/DC

How Do We (Party) by Rita Ora

Shake it Off by Taylor Swift

Welcome to New York by Taylor Swift

Heart of Gold by Birdy

Been a Son by Nirvana

Whiskey in the Jar by Thin Lizzy

She's a Rebel by Green Day

Here I Go Again by White Snake

Little Wing by Jimi Hendrix

Sweet Home Alabama by Lynyrd Skynyrd

Wonderful Tonight by Eric Clapton

Call Me Maybe by Carly Rae Jepsen

I Gotta Feeling by The Black-Eyed Peas

Swing Swing by All-American Rejects

Good Riddance (Time of Your Life) by Green Day

Wake Me Up When September Ends by Green Day

D Major Songs:

Send My Love (To Your New Lover) by Adele

We Sink by Chvrches

Castle on the Hill by Ed Sheeran

Align by Nina Nesbitt

All is Now Harmed by Ben Howard

Lithium by Nirvana

Settle Down by The 1975

Home by Gabrielle Aplin

Grow Up by Paramore

Wake Up by Rage Against the Machine

Hysteria by Muse

Under the Bridge by Red Hot Chili Peppers

Times Like These by The Foo Fighters

Only Girl (In the World) by Rihanna

Love Story by Taylor Swift

Summer of '69 by Bryan Adams

Hey There Delilah by The Plain White Ts

E Major Songs:

Break My Heart by Hey Violet

Don't Tell Me by Avril Lavigne

All I Ask by Adele

Piano by Ariana Grande

Ain't it Fun by Paramore

Basket Case by Green Day

Buck Rogers by Feeder

Back in Black by AC/DC

Sex on Fire by Kings of Leon

Pour Some Sugar on Me by Def Leppard

Midnight Memories by One Direction

Fat Lip by Sum 41

I Believe in a Thing Called Love by The Darkness

F Major Songs:

Ain't No Rest for the Wicked by Cage the Elephant

I'm Not the Only One by Sam Smith

Blank Space by Taylor Swift

What's My Age Again by Blink-182

Party in the U.S.A. by Miley Cyrus

Still into You by Paramore

The Wind Cries Mary by Jimi Hendrix

The House of the Rising Sun by The Animals

Bed of Roses by Bon Jovi

Scar Tissue by Red Hot Chili Peppers

Just the Way You Are by Bruno Mars

More by Preston Hoffman

Discover all books from the Music Best Seller Series by Preston Hoffman at:

bit.ly/preston-hoffman

Book 1: *Music Theory*

Book 2: *How to Read Music*

Book 3: *How to Play Guitar*

Book 4: *How to Play Ukulele*

Book 5: *How to Play Piano*

Book 6: *How to Play Chords*

Book 7: *How to Play Scales*

Themed book bundles available at discounted prices:

bit.ly/preston-hoffman